UNDERSTANDING RESEARCH IN COUNSELLING

GRAHAM BRIGHT AND GILL HARRISON

Series editor: Norman Claringbull

Learning Matters
An imprint of SAGE Publications Ltd 1
Oliver's Yard
55 City Road
London EC1Y 1SP

SAGE Publications Inc.
2455 Teller Road
Thousand Oaks, California 91320

SAGE Publications India Pvt Ltd
B 1/I 1 Mohan Cooperative Industrial Area
Mathura Road
New Delhi 110 044

SAGE Publications Asia-Pacific Pte Ltd 3
Church Street
#10–04 Samsung Hub
Singapore 049483

Editor: Luke Block
Development editor: Lauren Simpson
Production controller: Chris Marke
Project management: Diana Chambers
Marketing manager: Tamara Navaratnam
Cover design: Wendy Scott
Typeset by: Kelly Winter
Printed by Henry Ling Limited at
The Dorset Press, Dorchester, DT1 1H

MIX
Paper from
responsible sources
FSC® C013985
www.fsc.org

Library of Congress Control Number: 2013946210

British Library Cataloguing in Publication Data

A catalogue record for this book is available from the British Library

ISBN 978-1-44626-010-4
ISBN 978-1-44626-011-1 (pbk)

Contents

Foreword

Historically, many counsellors and psychotherapists have claimed to see little value in research. Their belief was that therapy is essentially an art – it could never be a science. Indeed, the traditional anti-science lobby in the helping professions has long maintained that the essential professional knowledge underpinning therapy's practices, and the necessary ways of professionalism being demanded from its practitioners, were somehow beyond investigation. Such allegedly numinous ways of knowing and such supposedly ineffable personal qualities did not need explaining; indeed, they could not be explained – they just 'were'. For such self-proclaimed therapeutic purists, research could never have any relevance. Put simply, for them it was not the business of 'proper' therapists.

Of course, what those research-deniers failed to notice was that therapists have always been, and still are, practitioner-researchers. They acquire new knowledge from books and journal articles; they test new therapeutic approaches; they attempt to find out what makes their clients tick; they try to discover the best ways of helping troubled people. In other words, they theorise, they investigate, they draw conclusions and they critically evaluate their ever-evolving ideas. All counselling and psychotherapy practitioners, whether they realise it or not, routinely carry out research every time they read a book, meet a new client or review an existing case.

Fortunately, any lingering anti-research ethos in the talking therapies is fading fast. Few, if any, of today's opinion formers in counselling and psychotherapy would deny the vital part that research plays in their profession. The sum of the research-based evidence to date is that counselling and psychotherapy contributes positively and effectively to the human condition. Far from exposing the talking therapies to irrelevant scientific evaluation and far from crudely demystifying them, what research actually does is to produce new learning that helps practitioners to better themselves and promote their calling.

This book's chief authors, Graham Bright and Gill Harrison, are very experienced counselling and psychotherapy teachers and practitioners. They have the depth of understanding and the breadth of knowledge to explain with authority just why gaining an understanding of the research process is a vital task – an essential responsibility – for all counsellors and psychotherapists because it teaches, underpins and promotes personal and professional development.

Written by practitioners, for practitioners, this book provides step-by-step guidance that shows readers how to carry out their own research and how to critically evaluate the work of others. What Graham and Gill illustrate within these pages is that research, no matter how worthy or vital, is not just of relevance to academics. Research is just as important to practising therapists too.

For counsellors and psychotherapists, research is a way of learning all that they can about their clients, their profession and themselves. Further, the wider research audience (and that is all of us) must learn how to critically evaluate both researchers and their findings. We need to be able to assess the researchers' objectivity, the quality of their work, and the significance of their conclusions. This means that when we are weighing up a piece of research, we need to find out who its advocates are and the circumstances under which they operated. What is the background to their work? What is being said? Who says so? Why do they say it? When did they say it? Where did they say it? In other words, in order to properly evaluate counselling research we must put the research, the researchers, the findings, and even the research users into context.

As researcher-practitioners, counsellors and psychotherapists are continually either carrying out their own enquiries or evaluating other people's investigations. In this book, Graham and Gill equip us with the essential tools to carry out these vital professional tasks most effectively. Moreover, the thinking skills that they help us to develop as putative researchers are useful well beyond counselling and psychotherapy; the pages within teach us how to be reflectively critical, a skill that is helpful in so many areas of both professional and personal life.

Dr Norman Claringbull
Series Editor
www.normanclaringbull.co.uk

About the authors and contributors

Graham Bright is Senior Lecturer in Education and Youth Work at York St John University. Previously he taught on a range of Teesside University-franchised programmes, including the FdA Counselling and the BA (Hons) in Therapeutic Counselling at Darlington and Redcar and Cleveland Colleges; he has practised as a counsellor with young people in a variety of settings. He is currently pursuing a PhD at Durham University, which explores comparisons and intersections between youth work and counselling, and the interplay between personal narratives, vocation and formation in these professions.

Norman Claringbull is the former Head of Counselling and Psychotherapy Studies at Southampton University. He currently combines his commercial consultancy work and private practice with ongoing research and various academic appointments at a number of UK universities. His website is www.normanclaringbull.com.

John AJ Dixon was a Lecturer in Counselling and Course Leader for Counselling at Redcar and Cleveland College. He taught on the Teesside University-franchised FdA Counselling and the BA (Hons) Therapeutic Counselling, and previously worked as a couples and family counsellor for Relate. He maintains some private training commitments and currently holds a full-time counselling position in the NHS.

Christopher Hall is programme leader on the Teesside University franchised FdA Counselling and FdA Working with Children and Young People at Darlington College. Previously, he taught on the BA (Hons) Therapeutic Counselling and BA (Hons) Education Studies. Chris is participating in research with Durham University examining adults' experiences of returning to further education. He maintains practice through Herriot Hospice Homecare and North Yorkshire County Council's Staff Care Network and is an MBACP Counsellor.

Gill Harrison currently teaches on a range of Teesside University-franchised programmes, including the FdA Counselling and the BA (Hons) in Therapeutic Counselling at Redcar and Cleveland College. She is also a visiting lecturer in Counselling at the University of Hull's Scarborough Campus. Gill's main research interest is in personal and professional development in counselling training for which she is currently refining her own PhD research proposal. She maintains a small private counselling and clinical supervision practice and is a Registered MBACP (Accred) Counsellor.

Introduction

Graham Bright

The counselling world faces increasing pressure to become research-engaged and research-informed. No longer is this confined to those perceived to dwell in the higher echelons of academia; there is a call, and indeed a growing expectation, that all counsellors and psychotherapists get (and remain) research-involved. This can be seen in the significance that many qualifying courses place on research-embedded practice, and in the ways that student research is no longer viewed merely as an exercise in academic competence. Research must be rigorous, yet accessible and applicable to be meaningful and worthwhile. This book grew out of our wish to debunk the myths surrounding research for our students, most of whom engage with research evidence for the first time as part of their Foundation Degree, and for the many who advance to complete a piece of research themselves at undergraduate and Master's levels. The key idea that underpins the text is our belief in the clear correlation that exists between the processes involved in the practice of therapy, and research concerning what happens in that practice. The attributes and skills that therapists embody are at the very centre of effective research practice; this book aims to describe and enable that transferability.

In Chapter 1, John Dixon and I set the scene by asking 'Why research?' Research is defined, and its growing interrelationship with practice is examined. The chapter considers the reasons for increasing research-engagement; barriers to and readers' feelings about research are explored with a view to making the research process less frightening and more accessible.

In Chapter 2, Chris Hall and I further these connections. We examine the notion of 'the use of self' in therapy and how this might be extended to research. We make connections to counselling training and consider professional formation in the context of wider personal development and argue ways in which practitioner research contributes to enhancing personal and professional identities.

In Chapter 3, John Dixon examines the distinctions and intersections between evidence-based practice and practice-based evidence. Consideration is given to how these ideas relate to different research paradigms and how they are used to construct different types of knowledge that when synthesised generate holistic insight.

In Chapter 4, Gill Harrison and I consider how we might tap into our own personal interests as a means of formulating an appropriate research question. In doing so, the chapter draws upon parallels regarding how insight is generated therapeutically, and suggests practical ways in which heuristic essence might enable the generation of researchable questions via an applied methodological framework.

In Chapter 5, I seek to unpack how knowledge is constructed by two major philosophical traditions: positivism and interpretivism. The chapter considers how different methodologies within these paradigms correspond to different elements of therapeutic practice. Links are made back to Chapter 3 to further discussion concerning the development of research knowledge in the profession.

In Chapter 6, I consider some of the practical concerns that many students have regarding research. This chapter seeks to aid the manageability of the task by offering some real-world advice regarding aspects such as time management. The second part of the chapter offers a discussion on ethics, and how ethical ideas might be applied to research practice.

In Chapter 7, John Dixon explores the value of different types of literature, and rationalises why it should be reviewed as part of a research study. This chapter offers excellent advice on how to conduct a literature search, how to construct and structure a review and ways in which sources might be synthesised to generate a 'critical backdrop' to the work.

In Chapter 8, Norman Claringbull, Gill Harrison and I further develop the ideas generated in Chapter 5 and offer application of two methodological approaches, one from each of the two major research traditions. The chapter seeks to connect the theory that underpins each methodology to its 'practice', thereby offering readers something of a 'step-by-step' insight into their application.

In Chapter 9, I examine the importance of ensuring the quality of research and consider how readers can best assure research validity in order that their work stands up to scrutiny. The second part of the chapter seeks to recognise and enable reflection on readers' personal research journeys and to contemplate how they have shaped them both personally and professionally. Suggestions regarding dissemination are discussed and readers are encouraged to ask 'What's next?'

We trust that you will find *Understanding Research in Counselling* both critically engaging and practically useful in your studies and continuing practice.

CHAPTER 1

Why research?

Graham Bright and John AJ Dixon

CORE KNOWLEDGE

By the end of this chapter, you will be able to:

- evaluate personal feelings about undertaking research;
- explain the benefits and limitations of research;
- trace key phases in the history of research in counselling and psychotherapy;
- relate key ideas in therapeutic practice to research;
- explain a relationship between counselling theory, practice and research.

The question 'Why research?' is one that doubtless crosses the minds, if not the lips, of many counselling students. For most, their initial foray into research comes as a requirement of counselling training, or the completion of a degree. There can, of course, be a gamut of thoughts and feelings experienced in approaching research, especially for the first time, and for many novice researchers the very idea of research can generate a sense of foreboding (Wheeler and Elliott, 2008). The question 'Why research?' therefore seems a reasonable one, particularly to the student who is *required* to complete research as part of his or her academic studies. Many students feel that research is more in the domain of their tutors, something undertaken in the dusty towers of academia (Etherington, 2009); and, while it is true that counselling and psychotherapy (terms we shall use inter-changeably) require academics to continue to produce quality research, engaging *practitioners* in research about therapy enables different, yet equally valuable, often more personal, and potentially more grounded, perspectives to be generated (McLeod, 1999). Practitioner research therefore offers the prospect at least of greater immediacy and potential learning to be generated between the researcher and his or her material, *since it is **they** that reflect on **their** work to identify what is needful* (du Plock, 2010, p127; emphases added).

This book aims to allay potential fears about research that readers might experience, to explore and make manageable research processes, and in doing so free readers to engage their research curiosity (Wheeler and Elliott, 2008). In this chapter, we contend that there are numerous reasons why counselling practitioners should participate in research about therapy as part of a process of *ongoing* personal and professional development. For the practitioner, the opportunity to engage in research is one that can enable critical, personal reflection about therapeutic theory, processes and outcomes in ways that offer the potential development of understanding about therapy in more holistic and systematic ways.

ACTIVITY 1.1

- Write down your personal thoughts and feelings about approaching research. Reflect on where these responses come from.
- Share your thoughts with a group of your peers and with your tutor/research supervisor.

REFLECTION POINT

- What do the thoughts and discussions you have had in response to Activity 1.1 tell you about you as a potential researcher?
- Whatever your response to this question it perhaps offers clues about the support or guidance you might want to seek out on your research journey. Take the opportunity to discuss this with colleagues and tutors/research supervisors.

The history of therapy as we understand it from modern times since the emergence of Freud has created a myriad of ideas and perspectives about the human condition and on systems of helping. It is not the purpose of this book to examine these developments in depth; however, it is important to note that, irrespective of any particular therapeutic school to which counsellors may adhere, the history of anything (including therapy), and the social conditions within which ideas arise and develop, play a part in how we construct meaning and identity, and the personal and professional attachments we give to them, and that therapeutic allegiances are no different. Research in its different forms is therefore central to and entwined with the historical development of therapy itself. Freud, it is recorded, would gather therapists to examine their therapeutic work with patients in a manner that sought to elucidate key therapeutic ingredients. The 1920s and 1930s saw the emergence of initial pre- and post-therapy *experimental designs* (Timulak, 2008, p11) that assessed client outcomes. Carl Rogers' work in the 1950s included tape-recording therapeutic interventions and using Interpersonal Process Recall (IPR) to enable both therapist and client to examine the essential ingredients of the encounter that were both helpful and unhelpful to the therapeutic process (ibid.). Therapy then is built on a long tradition of research designed to both quantify and qualify measurable therapeutic benefits as outcomes, and calculate the efficacy (production of desired effects) of therapy compared with alternative interventions. These forms of outcome research together with process research, which seeks to evaluate key therapeutic ingredients in the process of assisting clients, have become essential for understanding and justifying practice.

Claringbull (2010, pp14–16) identifies four phases to counselling research, encapsulated in Table 1.1. (Some of the terminology in Table 1.1 may be unfamiliar, but will be developed in subsequent chapters.)

Phase	Period	Key question	Key methods
1	1940–1960s	Does therapy work?	Measuring therapeutic intervention against control group outcomes.
2	1960s–1980s	How does therapy work?	Greater emphasis on counselling process research using both quantitative and qualitative methods.
3	1980s–present	Is therapy cost-effective?	Emphasis on quantitative methods that measure the effectiveness of therapy versus alternative drug-based or psychiatric interventions.
4	Present–future	What help should we give to those experiencing emotional and psychological difficulties? Is therapy more or less cost-effective than other forms of intervention?	The rise in randomised controlled trials (RCTs) and meta-analytical approaches (which encompass both quantitative and qualitative analysis) designed to discover the most appropriate and cost-effective forms of therapy for particular client groups or 'conditions'.

Table 1.1: Four phases of counselling research

THE RELATIONSHIP BETWEEN RESEARCH AND THEORY

Theory is essential to how we understand therapy; it provides a foundation for therapeutic work, which to some degree will be evidenced in both research and practice in order to provide ongoing evidence bases for its growth. The development of theory gives practitioners a place to 'hang their hat', a mechanism for explaining and even justifying practice. Such justificatory positions are both helpful and flawed. They are supportive in enabling the grounding of practice in a framework that assists in understanding clients and the distress they experience, but are flawed in restricting therapy to consider such issues from singular, limited and affixed positions. Perhaps in thinking about your own training as a counsellor particular ideas were held sacrosanct, not to be challenged. It is possible to trace such ideas and perspectives back to the origins of different therapeutic schools, where protagonists were keen to explain and justify particular values and approaches in working with clients and create empirical bases for doing so. One need only think about the infamous 'Gloria' recordings, which can now be found freely on the internet, as a case in point. Here we see three of the most eminent therapists of the twentieth century (Albert Ellis, Carl Rogers and Fritz Perls) not only working with a client, but seeking afterwards to explain and justify the theoretical ideas that underpinned their practice. We have many reasons to be thankful to these and other therapeutic pioneers in developing theory, research and debate in counselling and psychotherapy; yet there is also a sense in which the development of and allegiance to the rather rigid therapeutic schools (or perhaps more accurately *schoolism[s]* (Cooper and McLeod, 2011, p1)) that have ensued have led to forms of competition, tribalism and entrenchment. Timulak notes that counselling research:

> . . . *involves many stakeholders. Among them founders of different therapeutic approaches. They, as well as the therapists trained in their respective approaches, are substantially interested in having their approach empirically validated so that they can gain security in the therapy market.*
> (2008, p15)

Here an open-minded approach to research is crucial. As therapists, we desire to help clients, and want to understand how best to assist them, but perhaps we risk doing so through singular or narrow therapeutic lenses.

The rise of meta-analytical processes, which synthesise results from independent research findings, has provided the profession with significant data in assisting the development and justification of practice with particular client groups and issues (Cooper, 2008; Timulak, 2008). Yet herein lies a problem. Therapy, notwithstanding particular nuances of theoretical orientation, is about *human* encounter, of understanding and celebrating the *uniqueness* of each individual client. The danger, however, in the drive to prove the value of therapy through data analyses about underlying client pathology and corresponding 'treatment' merely generates statistical likelihoods, and modulates the humanity of the actual client with whom the therapist works. Cooper puts it this way:

> *What use is it, for instance, to know that anxious clients, on average, respond well to cognitive restructuring techniques? This tells us nothing about what might be helpful for the one individual client in front of me?*
> (2010, p183)

Research should therefore inform, but not dictate, therapeutic practice.

Research then offers the promise of being an emancipatory practice, one that affords space for different viewpoints and perspectives on the experiences, processes and outcomes of counselling to be described and analysed through a range of research methodologies; and it is these processes that contribute to the ongoing tapestry of what therapy has been, is and may become (Dallos and Vetere, 2005). Here the voices of different stakeholders – therapists, supervisors, trainers, counselling agencies, those who refer clients to therapy, funders and, perhaps above all, clients – can enrich our understanding of the realities of therapy, and how it might be shaped. It is in truly hearing the client's voice that we are able to collaboratively sustain inquiry and rehumanise therapy.

The British band, Manic Street Preachers, entitled their 1998 album *This Is My Truth Tell Me Yours*. Like the album title, research, whether investigating client experience directly or as chorused through the voices of counsellors, should enable ongoing and different 'truths' about the nature and experience of therapy to be played out and interpreted in ways that continue to shape our understanding. Research has the power to re-engage us with the reality of client experience, to liberate practitioners from unfounded psychotherapeutic canon and transport practice through the vehicle of empirical processes from narrow, entrenched and essentialist positions to more fluid, progressive and helpful ways of thinking (Cooper and McLeod, 2007, 2011). Knowledge about counselling and psychotherapy therefore should never become *fixed, dogmatic and immutable* (McLeod, 2007a, p3). Indeed, Dallos and Vetere extend this argument for continuous probing and critical thinking about the nature of therapy by stating: *researchers should dare to question fundamental certainties and dominant fashions in psychotherapy practice* (2005, p11). By engaging in research, each of us is able to draw on, and contribute to, the building of knowledge on which counselling and psychotherapy can continue to be understood, developed *and* justified.

All of us bring our own ideas, garnered through a range of experiences, including counselling training, practice and supervision, to the process of research. All of us hold particular philosophical positions about and beyond therapy, and it is critical that we examine the ideas we explicitly and, more often, implicitly hold in order that the research we engage with is rigorous and transparent, and pursues 'truth' as both an open space and as an objective direction. Counselling practice therefore does not occur in a vacuum. It is a dynamic process informed by theory, clients and practitioners. Each of these factors continues to influence the ongoing development of how we understand the others. Continuous research provides the proper empirical basis to understand these dynamic processes in order that the profession and its practitioners advance praxis in ways that are ethical and effective. Research becomes an integral vehicle through which knowledge about therapy can be co-created, with contributions from others used to enable processes of deepening and ongoing reflexion (Hedges, 2010), which hold the power to offer transformative ways of thinking about ourselves, our clients and our practice.

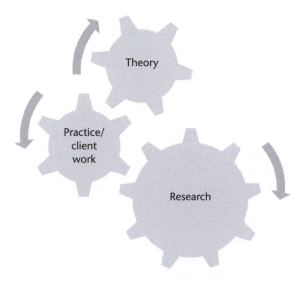

Figure 1.1: Understanding how research informs the praxis relationship

Figure 1.1 demonstrates the interlinking relationship between theory, practice and research. Theory informs practice, which in turn is informed by research. Practice tests the application of theory and informs our thinking about areas for development in theoretical knowledge. Questions that arise from practice inform research, which in turn informs theory and practice.

ACTIVITY 1.3

- What assumptions about therapy, therapeutic practice and work with client issues and groups do you bring with you to research?
- What informs these assumptions? How open are you to having therapeutic assumptions challenged as part of the research process?
- Consider how these challenges might impact on your professional or personal identity. Record these reflections in your research diary.

As we have discussed earlier in this chapter, research is necessary too for pressing and pragmatic reasons, in serving *as a justifier of therapeutic endeavour* (Timulak, 2008, p3; emphasis in original). Claringbull (2010) acknowledges that it is an exciting, yet challenging, time to be a therapist. Arguments around the future direction of counselling and psychotherapy ensue, and those commissioning therapeutic services need to be continually made aware and convinced of its efficacy, and the public assured of its helpfulness. Research therefore assists counsellors and psychotherapists to *communicate with others about their work, and to help consumers understand the value of what they do* (Cooper, 2008, p3). Counselling and psychotherapy's star continues to rise, and there is today widespread acceptance of its place in the fabric of society. Therapeutic interventions are increasingly in demand; however, with demand comes responsibility, greater requirements for accountability and the need for professional transparency (Corrie, 2010). The combination of these factors has led to increasing professionalism and professionalisation within the sector. Indeed, McLeod notes that there is a *tendency for professions to define themselves around a distinct knowledge base* (1999, p1). Research therefore plays a central role in assuring the ongoing place of counselling as a *profession*, which is accepted and valued by those responsible for commissioning services and by the wider public. Research also serves to advance, challenge and assure practitioners' professional identities. The resultant thirst for knowledge about therapy in an increasingly managerialist world is further heightened in times of economic austerity, when there is an increased requirement to justify 'what works', in order to ensure the value of therapy in comparison with other interventions. It is these different needs for knowledge about counselling and psychotherapy that *elevate research findings to the heart of the therapeutic endeavour* (Corrie, 2010, p44).

RESEARCH AND ETHICAL PRACTICE

As practitioners, we should be deeply committed in practice and active reflection to the application of ethical principles in our desire to help clients live more fulfilling lives; research enables this. Indeed, the British Association for Counselling and Psychotherapy (BACP) *Ethical Framework for Good Practice in Counselling & Psychotherapy* places research at the centre of the development of ongoing ethical practice:

> *The Association is committed to fostering research that will inform and develop practice. All practitioners are encouraged to support research undertaken on behalf of the profession and to participate actively in research work.*

> (BACP, 2010, para. 36)

Table 1.2 (adapted from BACP, 2010) examines how research fosters ethical action in therapy.

Just as ethics inform clinical practice, they also play a central role in the research process. The BACP produces guidance on ethical practice in research and information sheets that are useful for professional practitioners and counselling students undertaking research projects. Table 1.2 makes links to the 'ethical principles' underpinning counselling practice, but these are only part of the wider ethical considerations when undertaking research and are the subject of later chapters in this book. (We recognise that there are other professional bodies that represent counsellors and psycho-therapists, and students may wish to seek advice from their tutors about the professional body suitable for their courses.)

ACTIVITY 1.4

- Go to the British Association for Counselling and Psychotherapy website (www.bacp.co.uk) and have a look under the 'student' section for further advice on research. If you are not a member of the BACP it may be worth speaking to your tutors about student membership or exploring if the professional body with which your course is affiliated produces research materials to support students.

NB: The BACP produces a series of information sheets for student members that can be useful when thinking about research.

Ethical principle	Definition	Application to research
Fidelity	Honouring the trust placed in the practitioner.	Clients who are often vulnerable, by virtue of coming for therapy, place trust in the therapist and in the helpfulness of therapy.
Beneficence	A commitment to promoting the client's well-being.	Therapy exists to be helpful; professionals need to actively engage in understanding what might be of benefit to clients.
Non-maleficence	A commitment to avoiding harm to the client.	Research enables us to consider experiences of therapy and therapists, in ways that give insight about practice that might be unhelpful or even harmful to particular client groups.
Justice	The fair and impartial treatment of all clients and the provision of adequate services.	Properly constructed research provides an empirical basis for the development of services.
Self-respect	Fostering the practitioner's self-knowledge and care for self.	Research encourages practitioners to reflect on themselves and therapeutic practices in ways that extend personal and professional knowledge.
Autonomy	Respect for the client's right to be self-governing.	Research enables clients to make informed choices about therapy.

Table 1.2: Research and ethical action in therapy

THERAPY AND SUPERVISION AS RESEARCH

Humans are naturally curious creatures. On an everyday basis we are concerned with understanding the world around us, and navigating it through our interactions with others. Over time we have built up diverse systems of inquiry – ways of perceiving and understanding different aspects of reality. Our quest for insight can be seen in the education system, watching television, reading newspapers, using social media on the internet and in the nuances of our daily interpersonal communication. Our natural curiosity, whether consciously processed or not, casts us in the role of detective. Counselling is at its core an investigative process, where therapists work with clients in exploring from a myriad of therapeutic paradigms their stories, experiences and pathologies (du Plock, 2010). In psychodynamic counselling, the therapist works as a detective to enable the patient or client to make connections between past experiences and patterns of relating, with 'here and now' manifestations of those experiences through transferential dynamics. In cognitive behavioural therapy (CBT), the counsellor is concerned with understanding the formation of the client's schematic patterns and negative automatic thoughts (NATs) and works to help the client connect these to emotions and behaviours, encouraging the client to recognise, confront, challenge and change cognitive patterns. In the humanistic tradition, the counsellor seeks to join with the client in a relationally deep way (Mearns and Cooper, 2005), to understand the client and his or her story from the client's own perspective. In gaining deep empathic understanding of the client's incongruence, the therapist offers his or her own congruence as counterbalance, together with genuine and open acceptance of all the client is; the client him- or herself becomes more self-aware and self-accepting, and moves forward in his or her own healing process.

Supervision too provides rich opportunities for detective work; the supervisor and supervisee build a working alliance designed to examine different elements of what is happening in practice between counsellor and client. Time and space are given to investigate what might be happening in the counsellor's own life and development, his or her responses to the client and the issues that are being presented. Supervision affords dedicated opportunity for reflection about therapy, where it can often feel like the client is the invisible, yet key and highly tangible, witness in the dynamic client–therapy–supervision system (Carroll, 2008). Thus, supervision enables the counsellor and supervisor to deconstruct, examine and reconstruct the meanings and processes of therapy in a manner that elucidates it (Hawkins and Shohet, 2012). All human beings, therefore, are involved in ongoing research, and this is profoundly the case for the therapist in the ways he or she extends the 'use of self' (Wosket, 2011) in professional work with clients. Counsellors and psychotherapists then are well placed through training and experience to adapt and apply personal and professional skill sets to the realm of more formalised counselling research (du Plock, 2010).

DEFINING RESEARCH

While it is vital to consider human beings as naturally inquisitive and much human activity including therapy as investigatory, it is also important to define research as an academic activity more formally. Cooper helpfully offers this description: *[Research is] a systematic process of inquiry that leads to the development of new knowledge* (2008, p1).

It is important to pause here and think about some of the ideas that Cooper succinctly puts forward. First, we might be able to define 'systematic' as being ordered or planned and having some form of reasonable and justifiable method; research should not be random or haphazard. However, as we will explore later (in Chapter 5), the process of research does not necessarily have to adhere to unhelpfully rigid or fixed methods of collecting and analysing data, but should remain suitably flexible to enable pragmatism, and rigorous to ensure its validity. Denscombe frames it like this:

> *The process of putting together a piece of good research is not something that can be done by slavishly following a set of rules about what is right and wrong. In practice, the social researcher is faced with a variety of options and alternatives and has to make strategic decisions about which to choose.*

(2008, p3; emphasis in original)

Second, we might consider 'process' as a series of sequenced actions designed to meet an intended outcome. Third, the idea of 'inquiry' might relate to questions about therapeutic experience or outcomes, or exploration of particular theatres of therapeutic processes, practices and perspectives. The final point that we might identify from Cooper's definition is that research should develop new knowledge. This idea often creates a sense of panic-stricken-ness, particularly in novice researchers; the internal expectation here becomes that research must create something grand, unique or path-breaking. It is unlikely that the knowledge that is generated through much research at undergraduate or Master's level will give rise to uniquely brand-new knowledge or theoretical ideas about counselling, or that research likely to be completed at these levels will give rise to the 'fifth wave' in counselling and psychotherapy. That, however, is not to belittle the knowledge that *will* be generated by the research that students complete in deepening personal knowledge and reflection, which might be shared within agencies, counsellor networks, supervision, and in informing personal practice with clients. Each of us, as Sanders and Wilkins note, are *well able to contribute to the pool of knowledge on which our professions depend* (2010, p1). In extending Sanders and Wilkins' metaphor, engagement with new research is continually required in order to prevent stagnation in personal practice and in the profession more broadly. For some, the knowledge generated may also lead to their research being disseminated through publication, but whether this is an end result or not, the idea we wish to convey here is that practitioner research *does matter* and has the power to develop reflexive practitioners who, through the process of research, develop the capacity to be transformed by the knowledge *they* create.

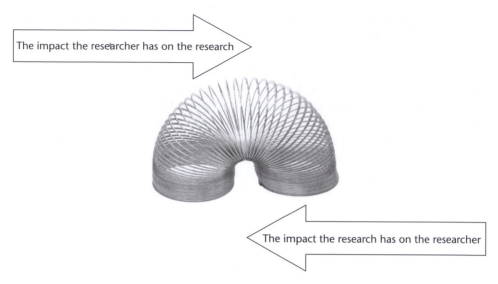

The impact the researcher has on the research

The impact the research has on the researcher

Figure 1.2: Reflexivity evaluates

RESEARCH, REFLECTION AND IDENTITY

Reflection is key in enabling therapists to get in touch with what is happening for them, for their clients and within therapy. The knowledge generated in active reflection offers the potential to transform practitioners both personally and professionally (Bager-Charleson, 2010; Hedges, 2010). Practitioner research is one way that offers the sustained time and space often denied to busy counsellors to think deeply and critically about particular theatres of practice in order to question constructed orthodoxies that risk becoming dogmatic mantras (McLeod, 1999; Dallos and Vetere, 2005; Cooper, 2010).

Research is, therefore, to be encouraged as a natural and welcomed component of therapeutic work; indeed, Wheeler and Hicks argue that it is a *foundation for practice* (2000, p537), where we are asked to consider and evaluate elements of our work (van Rijn, 2010). As we have already suggested, each of us brings to therapeutic practice and research innumerable experiences, ideals and beliefs that contribute to the maintenance and development of both our personal and professional identities. Of course, some aspects of these belief systems we may hold as more important or integral to us than others; and, in Activity 1.2, readers were asked to consider these ideas, and to record personal reflections. Deep learning has the power to be transformative; it can open our minds, challenge our thinking about life, our personal and professional biographies, and our beliefs about therapy and therapeutic practice, and can cause us to question, doubt, celebrate challenge or affirm what we know to be 'true'. Research as a process of deep and reflective learning has the potential to alter and recast both our personal and professional identities (Etherington, 2004). In approaching research, therefore, all of us must consider the degree to which we are willing and indeed able at a given point in time to be open to the potential challenges and changes that research may bring about.

REFLECTION POINT

- At the start of this chapter (Activity 1.1), you were asked to think about how you viewed and felt about the prospect of undertaking research and your views about yourself as a potential researcher. Having read this chapter, reflect on how your responses to this question might have changed.

CHAPTER SUMMARY

Here we return to the beginning of the chapter and reconsider the question 'Why research?' We hope that the chapter has begun to shape an answer to this question, which will develop as you continue to read through this book. While some of the language and terminology introduced so far might be unfamiliar to you, the ideas expressed will be developed to expand your thinking in later chapters.

The skills required to undertake research are formalised versions of many of the skills that counselling practitioners already possess. For example, asking peers, colleagues and friends for opinions on topics of interest will provide you with a range of responses (data) that you informally use (analyse) to draw your own conclusions. While there are differences in the philosophical and methodological processes involved in conducting research, you are not required to be an expert in every area of research methodology and data analysis, rather in developing competence in areas that fit your particular research interests.

In counselling and psychotherapy research, practice is central to what is often explored. The clinical work you have done with clients may have raised questions about your own practice, which may have begun to sow a seed for a research topic. Whether you are questioning the efficacy of your theoretical approach or considering the most appropriate way to respond to particular client issues, it is likely that research can be used as a tool to investigate these areas further. The key to successful research is discovering where your passion lies, and what interests you.

So, 'Why research?' We hope that readers' responses become driven less by the requirements of an academic course of study, and are increasingly because of a passion for and interest in the development of counselling and psychotherapy practice.

SUGGESTED FURTHER READING

Cooper, M and McLeod, J (2011) *Pluralistic Counselling and Psychotherapy.* London: Sage.

A seminal text designed to challenge and engage readers about the future of therapy.

McLeod, J (1999) *Practitioner Research in Counselling.* London: Sage.

A fantastic and reassuring text written to help novice researchers; the first chapter is of particular relevance to the material discussed here.

CHAPTER 2

Practitioner research: a therapist's perspective

Graham Bright and Christopher Hall

CORE KNOWLEDGE

By the end of this chapter, you will be able to:

- analyse links between the evolving practitioner and the emerging researcher;
- evaluate how internalised values and beliefs are experienced, challenged and changed through personal development and clinical practice;
- appraise how practitioners engage with research to develop personal professional 'selves'.

In this chapter we aim to facilitate an understanding of the links between the evolving practitioner and the emerging researcher. This discussion is framed within the notion that practitioner-researchers (and therefore research) continue to be influenced by internalised values and beliefs, which are recurrently challenged and changed through exposure to clinical practice, theoretical concepts, ethical frameworks and personal experiencing. Such reflexive ideas are at the nexus of therapeutic research processes, and require practitioner-researchers to foster the same forms of reflective engagement with research as is generated through therapy itself. Reflective practitioner-researchers should therefore develop the capacity to engender the type of parallel relationship with research that they experience in the therapeutic role. Research, like work undertaken in the triadic (client–counsellor–supervisor) therapeutic system, has the power to foster ongoing and ever sharper processes of enlightenment and conscientisation. Practitioner-researchers therefore need to give themselves to research in the same way in which they commit themselves as counsellors to clients in therapy, and learning in supervision, in order that they can benefit as fully as possible (personally and professionally) from the research process. This is made more fully possible when the practitioner-researcher is able to explore and reflect upon often challenging individual values and beliefs.

PHILOSOPHY AND ITS RELATION TO BELIEFS AND MORAL QUALITIES

The founder of modern philosophy, René Descartes (1596–1650), argued the difficulty in connecting mind and body (Scruton, 1995). Howard (2000, p136) describes this as *mind-matter dualism*, arguing that, for Descartes, *the incorporeal soul is apparently what is more real, most important and which most quintessentially comprises of who we are* (ibid., p134).

Throughout counselling training, students are exposed to identifying, exploring and developing their own sense of self on physical, cognitive, emotional, sexual and spiritual planes. Rose and Worsley (2012) argue that therapists need to understand self through multiple lenses in order that different perspectives can be used to enable clients to gain insight into their own multiple personal constructs. Through personal development, therapists commence a deeper life-long journey of self-exploration of the *whole self* as opposed to the parts with which they are at greatest ease and most comfortable (Johns, 2012). Indeed, it is the facets of our being with which we are *least* comfortable that often cause counsellors the greatest concern in practice. We are challenged most perhaps when clients bring issues into the therapeutic relationship for which we are least prepared, or have been unwilling or unable to examine for ourselves. Here, the counsellor may deflect from focusing on the client, and express in supervision or personal therapy (or indeed continue to suppress) the need to access and explore his or her own body, mind and soul.

Rogers' identification of an individual's sense of self was through a set of nineteen statements or *propositions* (see Rogers, 1951, pp481–524). He purported that an individual's ability to develop an appropriate sense of self would determine whether the person becomes *fully functioning* (Rogers, 1967, pp183–96). Such a process requires engagement with the core self, not just acceptance of self-concept. According to person-centred theory, there is an ongoing tussle between an individual's organismic self and his or her self-concept (Mearns and Thorne, 2007). The organismic or 'real' self comprises those innate aspects of our being with which we are born (Rogers, 1967; Mearns and Thorne, 2007) and which cannot be changed or altered. The ways in which we respond and interact, however, are to some degree shaped by the relationships we form with others, especially those people who have been significant in our lives (Bowlby, 1998). Positive relationships with others are likely to make us more confident and self-reliant, and lead us to have a stronger sense of self-worth (Bowlby, 1998; Mearns and Thorne 2000). Merry (1999, p18) contended that Rogers did not see the 'self' as fixed, but as *fluid, tentative and open to change through experience*. Therefore, the self-concept and organismic self may not be too different. It is, however, implicit and explicit expectations, introjected values and conditions of worth that are placed upon us by significant others which we find most difficult to shed – if we ever do. Such conditions and values can often become so engrained that they form part of who we are, leading to an inner struggle to maintain them. More recent developments in person-centred theory have suggested the 'self' as multifaceted, rather than singular. Mearns and Thorne (2007, p33–4) have coined the phrase *configurations of self* to describe this idea, which they argue is *self-within-a-self*. Indeed, Ropers-Huilman and Winters contend that *The selves and identities that we might believe to be the most authentic and comfortable to perform are not unitary* (2010, p44). Exploring conditions of worth and introjected values enables the individual to engage in a process that more congruently aligns these diverse selves, and to make decisions about which values and ways of being are shed or retained. Through personal therapy, personal development and supervision we engage in relearning selves. This for the therapist is a necessary step in order to realise the goal of therapy – that of fostering genuineness in the counselling relationship.

Therapy, irrespective of the nuances of orientation, requires that we bring, offer and use ourselves to facilitate the client's process in a natural, yet deliberate way. This 'use of self' (Rowan and Jacobs, 2011; Wosket, 2011) means bringing all that we are – our personal narratives, our values, indeed our whole being – to each new therapeutic encounter, and to place ourselves at the disposal of the client in attempting to enable him or her to gain personal healing and insight on the journey towards a more enriching way of living. It is inevitable, therefore, that our own stories and experiences, and the ways in which we have constructed them influence our own sense and use of self. Not only do therapists engage in deep listening to, and knowing of, their clients, they bring in their use of self – a cultivated *intrapersonal* knowing through which their clients' material and meanings resonate. Counsellors need not only to know and cherish their clients; they must foster a capacity to know and cherish the self in all of its multifaceted glory and 'shame' for the sake of self *and* others (Mearns and Thorne, 2007). Knowing extends to understanding and accepting ourselves fully and multi-dimensionally in the here and now, while recognising the influence of experiences and people in some way shaping who we are in the moment. Who we are and the values we embody are in part at least shaped by our pasts. In putting ourselves at the disposal of our clients, we bring our being and that which has shaped us (sometimes in vivid colour and sometimes in painted shadows) into the room. In this way therapist and client share a communion of stories. Hedges (2010, p15) argues: *When we meet a client we enter and join their culture; our identities inter-mingle.*

We develop our 'narrative identity' from the stories others tell about us; we are literally entangled in stories at the interpersonal level. Such intertwining has the capacity to generate deeper knowing in the therapist and client; yet too it requires the therapist (and his or her supervisor) to remain sufficiently disciplined to examine in conscious awareness the ways in which different biographies and their resultant values might impact on therapeutic work. The capacity for reflexive awareness is therefore essential to practice; it enables us to consider *how our own cultural, theoretical, personal and linguistic assumptions impact on our work* (Bager-Charleson, 2012, p31).

ACTIVITY 2.1

Most of us will be able to recognise the influence of others on different aspects of our lives.

- Draw a personal timeline; identify those who have been influential in your life. In what ways have these people shaped you and your values?
- How have your own experiences of personal therapy and counselling training influenced your own sense of self?

For many therapists, the process of journaling is integral to their personal and professional development and practice. The written word provides a site of possibilities, a place to reflect and record thoughts and feelings, a space to generate personal narrative (Hall, 2012).

Personally reflexive writing is the seed of narrative and autoethnographic inquiry. It is good for the soul; it has the power to foster deeper knowing of selves, and ways in which we relate to others. It provides a roadmap of knowing, and enables visualisation of the intersections between self and others. It gives space to reflect on values and examine the interplay between personal being and professional practice (Bolton, 2010; Bold, 2012). Aveline, in a personally reflective piece on what informs his own therapeutic practice, notes:

> *At heart, the view that I am proposing is personal to me and reflects my philosophy in life as well as my evolved perspective on what is important in effective psychotherapy . . . To understand my tacit focus, I need to show how I have arrived at this point, sketching my formation as a therapist, identifying some of the people (therapists and researchers) who have inspired me . . ..*
>
> (2005, p155)

ACTIVITY 2.2

- Either write down words or draw a picture that describes the essence of who you are. How do you perceive these ideas about yourself have changed over time?

- What has brought about these changes? Now repeat this exercise to describe your therapeutic practice. What do you find most demanding or challenging about your clinical work?

UNDERPINNING VALUES AND BELIEFS ABOUT COUNSELLING

Our personal and professional selves are influenced by a range of values located in different domains. As such, who we are and how we practise as therapists is shaped by the spatial and temporal nature of our ever evolving society, the impact of political ideologies and professional bodies together with the cultures and practices of counselling organisations.

While our own values and beliefs are central to the development of configured selves (Mearns and Thorne, 2007), therapeutic practice is further informed by various sources of counselling ethics (e.g. legal frameworks, professional codes of practice and agency policies and procedures) (Bond and Mitchells, 2008; Mitchells and Bond, 2010); indeed, the British Association for Counselling and Psychotherapy's *Ethical Framework for Good Practice in Counselling & Psychotherapy* (BACP, 2013) offers practitioners a recommended code, which advises on ethical practice. Bond considered that this framework should be seen as a scaffold for ethical practice: . . . *it is a conceptual structure that has metaphorical similarities to the scaffolding used to enable people to work on buildings* (2000, p53).

As practitioners, we should continually consider our own values in relation to others' in order that we are able to interrogate aspects of our being and praxis in the landscape of evolving values across different domains. Reflexive engagement with different values in this way means that we are often challenged by having to meet the requirements of various policies and standards that may be at odds with our own personally held beliefs (Green, 2010). Should our self-concept be susceptible to external influence, we may find it difficult to stand by our morals, ethics and values when challenged.

REFLECTION POINT

Bernard Moss argues that *values are not only at the heart of* people work practice, *but they also constitute the life force that permeates every part of practice . . .* (2007, p1; emphasis in original).

- How would you describe your personal values?
- What are the values of the professional body to which you belong?
- What are the values of the organisation where you practise?
- To what degree do you think values across these different domains are compatible?
- What are the challenges here?

While we might consider much concerning values and beliefs to be 'grounded', they are not fixed, but rather grow and develop as individuals, organisations and societies change. The flexible certainty of values can only truly be known when they are tested or scrutinised by experience. Our values simultaneously shape and are shaped by experience; they provide a sense of constancy and change. Such juxtaposition was expressed by the Greek philosopher Heraclitus, who argued: *No man ever steps in the same river twice, for it's not the same river and he's not the same man.*

LINKING PRACTICE TO RESEARCH

So far in this chapter, we have sought to examine perspectives on the nature of self and considered ways in which we have been and continue to be shaped by relationships and experience. We have also discussed 'the use of self' as a way of explaining something of the therapist's role in therapeutic processes, and have begun to unpick the influence of different value domains on therapeutic work. We now turn our attention to the place of the therapist as practitioner-researcher.

Westergaard posits:

> *Every profession or academic discipline is dependent on research to ensure that practice is continually improving and that evidence is gathered to support the work and help to transform the practitioners' (and clients') experience.*

(2013, p176)

It is usually through embarking upon a counselling course at undergraduate or Master's level that practitioners are required to engage in a research project. This for many is a maiden voyage (Finlay and Evans, 2009). While daunting, this journey becomes a rite of passage that enables the practitioner-researcher to grow both professionally and personally. Indeed, Moran has argued that many practitioner-researchers recognise *the significance of research as part of their professional self-definition* (2011, p175). Those who emerge from counselling training with a highly developed sense of self often develop the greatest capacity for reflexivity, and become most effective and intuitive in practice. However, the challenge only begins here; research engagement is an integral way in which therapists can cultivate their ongoing personal and professional development through learning and discovery, while enabling emergent therapeutic identities (or selves) to be nurtured (Bager-Charleson, 2010). In this way, when counsellors engage in practitioner research, they gain a more potent professional construct of being a therapist, and of therapy (Moran, 2011). Without doubt, research is increasingly informing therapeutic work. McLeod (2013a) argues that, while reading others' research has the power to develop personal practice, it is only in undertaking research oneself that wider research becomes fully impactive.

Palmer et al. call therapists to:

> . . . step back and learn from experience . . . [contending that] we are often so involved in and committed to our daily counselling work, that we can be deeply suspicious of the capacity of the outcomes of research to challenge our accepted practice and thinking.
>
> (1996, p529)

BEING A THERAPIST – BEING A RESEARCHER

Many counsellors express anxiety about undertaking research, arguing 'I trained to help clients, not be a researcher.' Yet counsellors, like practitioner-researchers from across a range of social and helping professions, are engaged in a particular dialogical way of being and knowing. In this way, counselling practitioner-researchers have an advantage of synchronicity between significant aspects of their clinical practice and the processes involved in research.

Writing from an action-research perspective, McNiff (2013) argues that research should engage in processes that engender tangible co-constructed changes in the researcher's own or organisational practice as opposed to generating less applicable forms of knowledge that are more concerned with building grand theories. Practitioner research collects layers of inter-connected stories to inform praxis. Here, McNiff locates and reflects upon the practitioner-researcher's use of self in the dialogical co-construction of knowledge:

> The 'I' of research is concerned about contributing to the wellbeing of others in the relationship and developing the kinds of dialogical relationship that will let this happen. Collaborative working therefore becomes more than a 'we'; it is 'I' in dialogical relation with others, and others in dialogical relation with me and others.
>
> (ibid., p8)

Practitioner research becomes a site for active discovery; it is at its core a way of being with others, a co-constructed interaction that mirrors much about the shared space experienced in the therapeutic encounter, and the active-reflective learning processes we find in supervision. Practitioner research, like the therapeutic relationship, fosters particular embodied ways of knowing: and, as with therapy, it calls us to reflect and learn deeply and intuitively with, from and through others. Finlay and Evans reflect:

> *In research, as in therapy, we seek to build a bridge to the Other, using our own special awareness, skills, experience and knowledge. We reflect on the Other's stories while simultaneously analysing our own responses and the dynamics of the evolving relationship between us . . . many of the familiar clinical skills and interests of psychotherapists (such as interviewing skills, empathy, reflexive or intuitive interpretations and inferential thinking) are directly transferable to the research domain.*
>
> (2009, pp3–4)

As we have argued, conscious awareness of personal and professional values and the ways in which they have been, and continue to be, framed and influence our lives are central to the effectiveness of therapeutic research and practice. Practitioner research firmly locates the researcher within research. Engagement with counselling research demands that we bring ourselves to, and use ourselves in, processes of research. Values and experience drive heuristic forms of inquiry (Moustakas, 1990); therefore, explicit exploration of values and the voices that carry them is needed in order to fulfil the potential of what is possible. Banks argues that: *The hearts [values] of social scientists exercise a cogent influence on research questions, findings, concepts, generalisations and theories* (2010, p45). Just as in therapy, practitioner-researchers are required to know themselves and make that knowing appropriately explicit:

> *. . . researchers should know and be able to articulate who they are and what they believe personally, so that they may understand and acknowledge how these factors influence the research.*
>
> (Savin-Baden and Major, 2013, p68)

As with the therapeutic encounter, our values and experiences inevitably shape processes of research. Awareness of these influences enables the researcher to make clear adopted stances, to paint vistas of particular worldviews and to argue reflexively from particular positions (Hanley et al., 2013). It is for this reason that Langdridge emphasises the centrality of reflexivity as:

> *. . . the process by which researchers are conscious of and reflective about the ways in which their questions, methods and very own subject position*

. . . might impact upon the psychological knowledge produced in the research study.

(2007, pp58–9)

Interactions between social actors in any domain have the potential to bring about or exacerbate (intentionally or not) power differentials (Hearn, 2012). In many aspects of society power is wielded by the powerful over the powerless, by the 'haves' over the 'have-nots'. In thinking critically, most of us would be able to recognise such struggles in our own lives and communities. Therapy is no exception: a client coming for counselling is likely to be vulnerable in some way. The very act of help-seeking places the therapist in a position of power over the client; power differentials need to be recognised and mitigated or worked with psychotherapeutically. Power when enacted has the potential for good and harm; our use of power is an expression of our values, and unchecked can represent an unthinking wrecking ball.

Most forms of practitioner and action research are likely to involve us in relationships, which are in different ways a seat of power. Practitioner research should foster knowledge, but knowledge that is *co-constructed* (Finlay, 2011; McNiff, 2013). Practitioner-based research is not done to people or even with people; contributors become equals in the process, they are valued for their own humanity rather than for what they can contribute. In this way, power imbalances can be redressed. Clearly, as with therapy, ethical boundaries and responsibilities need to be considered, managed and beneficently enacted. Despite their divergent purposes the connections between therapeutic work and practitioner research are clear. Both are concerned with the development of knowledge generated through relational, intuitive and ethical ways of being. Practitioner research creates a *bridge* (Finlay, 2011, p7) between the high towers of empiricism and the *swampy lowlands* (Schön, 1983, p42) of practice. It connects our use of self through the relationships, attributes and skill sets that we engage in practice, with the processes of co-constructing knowledge that support our ongoing personal and professional development.

ACTIVITY 2.3

Refer back to Activity 2.2 where you examined the challenges of your own clinical practice.

- Where do you seek sustenance for, or 'answers' to, these challenges?
- How might research be useful in supporting your exploration of these issues?
- What answers would you like to find?

Case study 2.1

Here, one of us (Chris) reflects on his experience of practitioner research during his Master's degree (Hall, 2011):

Initially, I felt undertaking research a daunting prospect. However, I was reassured, encouraged and supported by my mentor to brainstorm any ideas that I might have. Subsequently, a theme began to emerge. Having recently completed a module in Drama Therapy I was intrigued by attire. In my counselling practice I am conscious of seeing the client as a whole person, not just as they present with issues or concerns, but how they present as a unique individual. The topic that emerged addressed my wish to focus on the uniqueness of the individual and how they present themselves through dress within therapy.

The research question which resulted was: '*Is How I Dress Who I Am?*' My aim through an individual case study was to discover whether a client is consciously aware of what they choose to wear in therapy, and whether those choices are linked to how they are feeling. Although the focus was to be on the individual's visual presentation, their foot attire and use (or lack of) jewellery, make-up, perfume and accessories were of importance. Indeed, I was hoping to discover if their whole dress could be linked to their feelings in the here and now. In discussion with my counselling peers and through reviewing the extant literature, I became aware of the lack of substantial research in this area.

I felt that understanding the richness of another's perspective was of real importance and therefore decided to approach the research from a phenomenological perspective. A semi-structured interview provided my co-researcher with the time and space to develop rich description of her experiences. The interview was recorded and later transcribed. Emerging themes were identified and analysed in relation to the participant's thoughts, feelings and meanings during the process of therapy. Analysis was furthered to consider how these experiences informed her choice of dress. Of course, it was not so straightforward, especially when I was informed that my co-researcher came to counselling straight from work, therefore was dressed in '*work clothes*'. Her choice of clothes was further informed by a workplace dress code which resulted in sartorial incongruence. In this way the participant expressed a conscious choice about how she dressed for work. '. . . *Everyone was so dreary and dull, so I bought some really dull clothes . . . to fit in . . . I am aware that what I wear is not who I am, what I wear is the function. It's the job . . . rather than me!*' Although she identified herself as being '*quite conservative*' in her dress, on the occasion we met she consciously chose to wear a cerise blouse and matching lipstick. She shared that she believes in colour therapy: '*I have a feeling that colours can influence mood . . . you have to be in a certain mood to put this on or that on . . . dress is really important and says a lot about you. Well it does to me!*' There appeared awareness on her part of the complexity of her own self-identity (Elliott, 2008), acknowledging for her that work clothes identified her job, not who she is.

I learned that the key to being a practitioner-researcher is to engage in research which is personally meaningful. There were moments when I wondered 'Why am I doing this?' especially when time became constricted. Engaging with a research supervisor throughout research was paramount. There were certainly times when being able to discuss my options with an experienced practitioner-researcher was significant in moving the research task forward. The completion of my research brought a deep sense of achievement. It also brought a shift – almost a greater completeness in my professional identity as a therapist; it deepened my own sense of inquiry about what I do in practice, enabling me to make more vivid connections between theory and practice, and practice and theory. It was only through the challenge of research engagement that I further discovered and developed a more 'whole' sense of my professional self. Although not necessarily a comfortable experience, it was certainly one which has made me aware that growth (for me) needs to continue, though it may be both painful and rewarding.

A PHENOMENOLOGICAL BRIDGE

Irrespective of approach, research is concerned with the generation of knowledge about phenomena. In Chapter 5, we examine a range of ways in which knowledge is constructed. For the time being, however, and in order to develop the bridgehead between research and practice, we focus our attention on phenomenological approaches that place personal *experience* centre-stage. Phenomenology considers meaning and how meaning is constructed through experience. Stewart (2005) posits that phenomenology focuses on the individual's conscious experiences rather than probing for underlying causes. Purists argue that rich description of lived experience is of greater importance than cause and interpretation.

However, the debate within phenomenology concerning whether description of experience and/or methods of interpretation should be used is considerable. Currently there is movement towards more interpretive, hermeneutic approaches (e.g. Interpretative Phenomenological Analysis (IPA)), which seek to embed and explain experience within specific contexts (Smith et al., 2009). IPA's phenomenological-hermeneutic roots (as we shall note later in Chapters 5 and 8) place equal emphasis on description and interpretation. Notwithstanding the detail of argument, it is the phenomenological researcher's role to facilitate exploration and discovery of the richness of experience and meaning, and to convey this as it is lived (Langdridge, 2007).

Phenomenology offers clear connections between therapeutic practice and research (Finlay, 2011). The counselling practitioner-researcher who adopts a phenomenological approach can *be* with the Other at the heart of the research in a way that mirrors much about the empathic engagement of therapy. As such, it is encouraging to note that these research methodologies, which draw on the same philosophical wells that nourish many counselling approaches (and which have informed the ideas of therapeutic pioneers such as Rollo May and Carl Rogers), are gaining multi-disciplinary kudos in the social sciences, and fostering new waves of practice-based research within caring professions such as counselling.

Our hope, therefore, in writing this chapter is that the practice–research gap that initially appears to overwhelm so many novice counselling practitioner-researchers may not feel so vast after all.

CHAPTER SUMMARY

This chapter has considered ways in which therapists bring and use themselves in therapy. We have evaluated the influence of personal narratives and experiences on the development of therapists' selves. We have argued the centrality of research in professional formation, and considered 'ways of being' and common values that connect the processes and practices of therapy with practitioner research.

SUGGESTED FURTHER READING

Finlay, L and Evans, K (2009) *Relational-centred Research for Psychotherapists.* Chichester: Wiley-Blackwell.

CHAPTER 3

Evidenced-based practice and practice-based evidence

John AJ Dixon

CORE KNOWLEDGE

By the end of this chapter, you will be able to:

- explain evidence-based practice and practice-based evidence;
- discuss the relationship between evidence-based practice and practice-based evidence;
- evaluate the contribution of qualitative and quantitative research to evidence-based practice.

Evidence-based practice is probably not completely new to you, although the terminology used may be unfamiliar. As a counselling student you will have been required to examine your practice through case studies and presentations. Indeed, a central part of much clinical training in counselling and psychotherapy requires some form of case presentation and a great deal of emphasis is placed on reflective practice. The rationale behind this form of assessment is about developing skills to enable you to explain why you work in the way you do, and to rationalise the approach you adopt. As your professional career develops you may move into the role of a supervisor of counsellors and psychotherapists; in this role you will not only be thinking about the basis for your own therapeutic work, but exploring the rationale behind the work of the counsellors you supervise.

Interpersonal Process Recall (IPR) is a useful supervision tool developed by Kagan (1980). It is designed to increase counsellors' awareness of their own practice through careful examination of therapeutic interactions. The idea is to create a climate where you can discuss openly with your supervisor what is happening in the session, so you can learn more about the client–counsellor relationship and the efficacy of your approach.

The process is as follows:

- negotiate with your clinical supervisor co-examination of a recorded counselling session (taking account of issues of client consent and confidentiality);
- in clinical supervision, review the video recording of the session, reflecting on your thoughts and feelings and what is happening for the client as the session progresses;
- take turns with your supervisor, stopping the tape at key points you wish to reflect on, or at points the supervisor wishes to ask questions about;
- at the end of the session, reflect on your key learning from the process.

ACTIVITY 3.1

As a means of thinking about your approach to practice and to examine the reasoning behind your therapeutic interventions, negotiate an IPR session with your clinical supervisor. After the IPR exercise consider the following questions.

- What did you notice about your rationale for the interventions used?
- To what extent did theoretical knowledge, clinical experience, clinical guidelines and research inform therapeutic work?

The essence of evidence-based practice is about being able to define and justify clear reasons for your approach to therapy in order to deliver the best service for clients and for the agencies or organisations in which you work. Sackett et al. discuss evidence-based practice in medicine, and provide probably one of the most cited definitions of the approach. It is, they argue:

> . . . the conscientious, explicit, and judicious use of the current best evidence in making decisions about the care of individual patients. The practice of evidence based medicine means integrating individual clinical expertise with the best available evidence from systematic research.
>
> (1996, p2)

This definition is useful as it covers a number of key elements relevant to counselling and psychotherapy practice. To be conscientious means that we have a commitment to do the right thing. This can be linked to the ethical principles of fidelity, beneficence and non-maleficence (BACP, 2013). Doing the right thing means that we make therapeutic decisions that place the client's trust in us as the foundation of our work, and that we apply approaches to client work that seek to *promote the client's well-being [and] avoid harm to the client* (ibid., p3).

To be explicit and judicious requires counsellors to be able to clearly explain why they adopt a particular approach and to make considered judgements. Initially, this is likely to be based on what you have been taught as part of your counselling training and on a belief in the approach you are applying. As your experience grows in working with clients, it is likely your approach will become informed by what you have found works in practice with particular clients or client groups, and from discussion with clinical supervisors (Cooper and McLeod, 2011; Lapworth and Sills, 2011; O'Donnell and Vallance, 2012). However, there is also a need to consider agency policies and procedures as well as clinical guidance and research literature. Many students can find the latter (looking at research literature) a somewhat daunting task, but as we shall see this is an important element of evidence-based practice.

JUDICIOUS USE OF CURRENT BEST EVIDENCE

ACTIVITY 3.2

- Spend a few minutes considering what constitutes evidence for the efficacy of counselling. Note down the ideas that you come up with.
- How prominently did research appear in your notes?

What constitutes 'current best evidence' is a somewhat contested issue in counselling and psychotherapy. In medicine and increasingly in counselling and psychotherapy the approach to 'best evidence' has come from quantitative research in the form of randomised controlled trials (RCTs) and systematic reviews (Bower, 2010; Cooper, 2011). This poses some difficulties for many counselling researchers who prefer qualitative research approaches that seek to capture the essence of therapist or client experience, and offers some interesting arguments against blanket acceptance of RCTs as the only source of 'best evidence'. Quantitative research, however, involves large-scale measures and often a comparison between different variables and is seen by the scientific and particularly the medical community as the favoured approach to research (see Chapter 5 of this volume for a fuller discussion of qualitative research methods and RCTs).

RCTs are regarded by the medical profession and by the National Institute for Health and Care Excellence (NICE) as the 'gold standard' of evidence as to whether a treatment is effective. NICE uses the outcomes of RCTs to inform the guidance it produces for clinicians when deciding treatment options. In terms of counselling and psychotherapy practice, NICE guidelines have played a major part in the rollout of the UK Government's

Improving Access to Psychological Therapies (IAPT) agenda and the promotion of CBT as a treatment of choice for anxiety and depression.

Rather than posing an argument for or against RCTs, which is beyond the scope of this chapter, it is perhaps more useful to look at the range of possible evidence that informs evidence-based practice. Roddam and Skeat (2010), after Sackett et al. (1996), write about the role of evidence-based practice for speech and language therapists, and suggest three fundamental elements that constitute it:

- research evidence;
- the experience of the clinician;
- consideration of clients' circumstances and preferences.

Each of these elements will be explored in some detail.

RESEARCH EVIDENCE

Research evidence in counselling and psychotherapy is a broad category but primarily consists of qualitative research approaches. While RCTs are the current research approach of choice for policy makers in the statutory sector, Cooper (2011) advocates the need for more non-RCT evidence, while acknowledging the benefit of RCTs for counselling and psychotherapy. McLeod (2011a) supports this view and argues that there is a need for more non-RCT evidence to be generated from qualitative research approaches, particularly outcome studies (studies that focus on clients' experience of therapy and its impact). The issue here, however, seems to be the availability of substantial data from qualitative research to support diverse therapeutic approaches to working with client issues.

McLeod (2011a) suggests that this may be due to a lack of practitioner research engagement. Indeed, it is the author's experience that counselling and psychotherapy students often seem daunted by undertaking research and perhaps this translates into a reluctance to conduct research in their practice once qualified. McDonnell et al. (2012) suggest that many practitioners want to engage with published research to see if it has relevance to their practice, but that training in research methodologies needs to be more fully integrated into counselling and psychotherapy courses. Widdowson (2012) also supports this view and offers a challenge to counselling and psychotherapy trainers, supervisors and researchers to make research and research findings more accessible and practice-relevant. The arguments are compelling, especially when McLeod (2011a) highlights that, of the hundreds of students who graduate from counselling and psychotherapy courses each year, it would only take a handful to begin contributing relevant outcome-based research studies to generate good evidence to further develop systematic reviews (a topic addressed later). Despite therapists being passionate about their work, there remains an unfortunate reticence or anxiety with many about conducting their own research.

ACTIVITY 3.3

- How relevant is research to your practice? Note down key points that come to mind.
- Now, regardless of your answer, how did this attitude to research develop?
- What do these views tell you about your overall response to engaging with research?

Systematic reviews of evidence

Conducting a systematic review is one way in which evidence of the efficacy of therapeutic approaches can be examined. A systematic review is in essence an in-depth exploration of literature on a given topic. They are typically used by NICE in constructing clinical guidelines. Aveyard and Sharpe outline some key features of systematic reviews.

- *There must be a clear method applied to sourcing and appraising relevant literature including criteria to establish what will be included and excluded from the review.*
- *The review must make a judgement on the quality of the papers selected excluding those regarded as poor quality (for example, those containing methodological weaknesses).*
- *The review must be thorough and include both published and unpublished works if relevant to the subject of the review.*
- *The review must bring together the findings of the papers which allows for 'new insight to be drawn from the summary of the papers that was not available before'.*

(2012, p55)

Systematic reviews have the advantage of taking a great deal of information about a given topic from reliable research sources and thereby provide a strong evidence base. Furthermore, qualitative and quantitative research can be included. Systematic reviews, therefore, appear to offer a wealth of untapped potential that synergises a broad range of literature to support the efficacy of different therapeutic interventions while meeting the challenge of generating wide-ranging evidence that is not grounded in RCTs (Cooper, 2011; McLeod, 2011a).

Here, counselling and psychotherapy practitioners can really engage with research and contribute to the evidence on which best practice can be based.

ACTIVITY 3.4

- The British Association for Counselling and Psychotherapy has published a number of systematic reviews exploring different aspects of therapeutic work. Spend some time on its website (www.bacp.co.uk) and download a systematic review; get a feel for the amount of research used to contribute to the review and its key findings.
- See if you can find a systematic review on a topic relevant to your practice and compare it to a general research paper. What are the key differences you notice?
- What impact might the review selected have on your practice?

NICE's website has links to a range of research papers and systematic reviews (NICE, 2013a), including a link to the Cochrane Library, a collection of databases on topics relevant to healthcare. Look at these to get a sense of the range of systematic reviews available that are relevant to counselling and psychotherapy (www.evidence.nhs.uk/nhs-evidence-content/journals-and-databases).

THE EXPERIENCE OF THE CLINICIAN

Although there is no legal minimum training requirement for counsellors in the United Kingdom, there is a variety of requirements of professional counselling and psychotherapy training providers in terms of the number of clinical hours students need to complete to achieve their qualification. The BACP (2009) 'gold book' standards for accreditation of counsellor training courses recommended 150 hours of supervised clinical practice as being the minimum required for qualification as a counsellor; however, this has been reduced to 100 hours following amendments to the gold book standards (BACP, 2012).

Regardless of the number of clinical hours completed to achieve qualification, newly qualified counsellors can experience challenges when starting out in practice. They may rely heavily on their relationships with supervisors when making clinical judgements and perhaps even desire supervisors to vicariously counsel their clients through the supervisory relationship. Initially, it is likely that most clinical judgement is based on the theoretical approach in which the counsellor has trained, rather than direct experience of working with particular client issues. While supervision remains an important feature of therapeutic work, as clinical experience grows, counsellors are likely to feel more confident in exercising their own judgement, utilising supervision for consultative support while developing an autonomous professional sense of self in decision making.

The nature of counselling and psychotherapy practice requires therapists to reflect on their work and operate within a professional ethical framework (Bond, 2010). Keeping up to date with developments in practice through regular continuous professional development and reading professional journals are ways in which counsellors and psychotherapists continue to develop their clinical experience alongside direct client work. Utilising clinical experience in making practice judgements is a challenging task when practice guidelines continually change in light of new evidence and changing organisational demands. Practitioners work within a competitive therapeutic marketplace that demands the effectiveness of therapy to be evidenced, and this can place a strain on how counsellors and psychotherapists feel about face-to-face work with clients.

However, in line with evidence-based practice, practitioners need to make effective clinical decisions that take account of current best evidence in providing therapy to clients. It is not a case of 'we've always done it this way'; there must be scope for change, and this may mean that counsellors need to respond in ways that their initial professional training had not fully prepared them for. Counsellors and psychotherapists may therefore need to be prepared to undertake additional training and to be flexible in their approach. That said, evidence-based practice also means that practitioners need to think through the rationale for the way things are being done, and be prepared to question practice in the light of clinical guidelines and research evidence.

CONSIDERATION OF CLIENTS' CIRCUMSTANCES AND PREFERENCES

An ethical response to client work requires that the needs of the client are always at the centre of therapeutic work. The BACP (2013) *Ethical Framework for Good Practice in Counselling & Psychotherapy* clearly outlines this commitment in its description of the ethical principles of beneficence and non-maleficence. The needs of the client therefore cannot be neglected when following an evidence-based approach. Clinical guidelines, such as those offered by NICE for the treatment of depression (NICE, 2013b), may indicate a therapy of choice for responding to a particular client issue, but the client's preferences and circumstances still need to be considered. Assessments of suitability for counselling and psychotherapy that take into account the appropriateness of the approach offered to the client therefore need to be considered. When thinking about client preference in therapy, there is also a responsibility to ensure clients are fully informed about the services available to them. The idea of client choice is only truly effective if clients are fully informed and can make decisions based on accurate information about their treatment choices. This requires practitioners to be clear on what they can offer (which is likely to be influenced by organisational and resourcing constraints) and to support clients to access suitable services. Here, explicit and informed client consent to actively engage with therapy (which is an ethical requirement when making contracts for counselling and psychotherapy relationships) should be a concern (BACP, 2013).

Evidence-based practice is therefore not simply about applying what research and clinical guidelines say about what makes effective practice, it requires practitioners to exercise clinical judgement and take account of client needs in planning treatment approaches and designing services.

ACTIVITY 3.5

- Go to the National Institute for Health and Care Excellence website (www.nice.org.uk/CG90) and download a copy of the **quick reference guide** to the CG90 guidelines for the treatment and management of depression in adults (NICE, 2013b).
- Identify what the guidelines recommend in terms of psychological therapies for treating depression.
- Consider the approaches you offer when working with depressed clients.
- Consider how your practice fits in with the NICE guidelines.
- What evidence informs your approach?

PRACTICE-BASED EVIDENCE

A complementary approach to developing a more research and evidence-based approach to therapy is based on 'practice-based evidence'. This approach to research is often more accessible to practitioners as it involves collecting evidence from practitioners' day-to-day activities with clients. It is concerned with the client's experience of the therapy whether through qualitative or quantitative means.

Perhaps the most accessible (but least robust) way of gathering data from practice is through practitioners reflecting on their practice. This might, for example, involve the use of clinical supervision. Practitioners observe what seems to work well with clients and notice gaps in their practice. This may lead them to identify approaches or strategies that seem to be effective when responding to clients as well as noting areas for development, which they begin to address through a commitment to continuous professional development. Indeed, the commitment to undertake this kind of reflection is an ethical one and is based on a philosophy of continuing to develop practice for the benefit of clients. It is likely that, as clinical experience grows, practitioners will draw on a broader range of interventions and approaches to support clinical work. This process might be considered to be a form of practice-based evidence in that decisions about practice are based on the therapeutic experience of working with clients.

However, such an approach to practice-based evidence is limited and relies heavily on anecdotal assumptions that lack robust evidence for dissemination to a wider audience. Practitioners might share their insights with other therapists; this can be helpful in informing practice, but lacks methodological rigour. To be robust, therefore, practice-based evidence needs to be based on the application of research methodologies to understand or measure what happens in clinical practice.

ACTIVITY 3.6

Think about your own clinical practice – what might you be interested in?

- Understanding – what phenomena spark your curiosity?
- Measuring – what aspect(s) of your practice might lend themselves to some form of measurement?

Barkham et al. offer a useful description:

> . . . *practice-based evidence in relation to therapy is grounded in research findings derived from studies of various aspects of therapy practice and can be viewed as a real-world test of any particular psychological intervention or service delivery model.*

> (2010, p1)

There are a number of approaches to practice-based evidence; however, it is beyond the scope of this chapter to address each one, although further reading has been suggested at the end. Essentially, however, both qualitative and quantitative approaches to research can be part of the process of gathering practice-based evidence. Qualitative approaches often provide a wealth of in-depth information about clients' experiences of therapy and may play a useful role in the evaluation of therapeutic services; however, they also have their limitations as they often capture the views of relatively small groups of clients and, furthermore, take time to analyse. It is also worth considering what information qualitative research captures.

Generally, qualitative practice-based evidence focuses on the 'experience' of therapy (e.g. how the client feels about therapy), rather than the 'outcome' (which is more concerned with capturing how the client presents and progresses from one session to the next, and being able to monitor this from the start of therapy to its conclusion). Client 'experience' of therapy is nevertheless important and a valuable part of practice-based evidence; however, capturing this purely through qualitative means is limited.

A well-used method of gathering practice-based evidence is through the use of Clinical Outcomes in Routine Evaluation (CORE). This system of measures provides a tool through which practitioners can collect quantitative data on the 'process' and 'outcomes' of therapy. CORE also provides a snapshot of a client's current level of functioning, and therefore may provide some basis for therapeutic interventions. Mellor-Clark and Barkham (2012) provide a 'best practice' explanation of how CORE measures might be used; briefly, this involves clients completing questionnaires that attempt to provide an overview of their psychological well-being using a numerical score. This form of measure is particularly useful as it is fairly straightforward to adopt and implement and allows the collation of data from multiple practitioners within a service. While the individual practitioner can use the data to monitor client progress using clinical scoring, the larger data set gathered can be used to evaluate client progress across organisations as well as analysing the demographic data to uncover trends. Multiple services using CORE might pool their data to give a wider view of trends that could then feed into service development and evaluation, funding bids, enhancing training and engaging with policy issues relating to the provision of therapy. This form of data pooling does not have to be restricted to organisations, but could involve networks of individual practitioners through Practitioner Research Networks (PRNs).

ACTIVITY 3.7

Barkham et al. (2010) identify a number of PRNs that could be of value to practitioners and organisations interested in developing their use of practice-based evidence.

- Go to the British Association for Counselling and Psychotherapy website (www.bacp.co.uk) and look up the information sheets R17 (in the members' area). Identify which PRNs might be of interest to you or your organisation.

While CORE is a well-established measurement system, when thinking about practice-based evidence it is important to consider the most appropriate system of measures for the service being delivered. The aim of practice-based evidence is to gather information from practitioners' day-to-day work in order to inform and develop, and thereby enhance the evidence bases that underpin service provision.

THE RELATIONSHIP BETWEEN PRACTICE-BASED EVIDENCE AND EVIDENCE-BASED PRACTICE

Evidence-based practice and practice-based evidence are related and complementary concepts. As has been explored, practice-based evidence focuses on practitioners engaging in a process of gathering data on their day-to-day clinical work; this creates not only opportunities for evaluation of services but also scope to disseminate findings through practice networks. Opportunities are created as part of this process to engage in the publication of data in research studies. As information is shared through peer-reviewed research and publication, it reaches a wider professional audience, thereby growing the evidence base in order to increasingly inform the work of other practitioners and to influence clinical guidelines while highlighting further gaps in evidence. These gaps inspire practitioners to collect data from their work and to consider ways of enhancing research practice.

Evans et al. make an interesting point when they suggest that: *the PBE [practice-based evidence] paradigm should engage practitioners in the collection and ownership of data and in analyses of that data which can inform their practice* (2003, p375). Perhaps what should be added is that the analysis of such data is not only useful in informing the practice of individual counsellors or counselling organisations, but it becomes valuable data that influences the practice of other counsellors and psychotherapists, thus contributing to evidence-based practice.

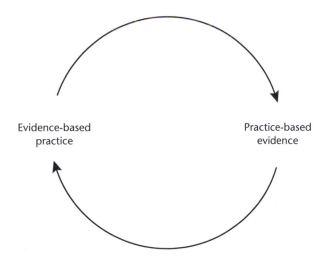

Figure 3.1: The relationship between evidence-based practice and practice-based evidence

CHAPTER SUMMARY

The link between research and practice is something that is becoming increasingly important in counselling and psychotherapy. Ultimately, funders of services providing psychological support want to know that money is being spent effectively, and look to therapies with a solid evidence base to provide this. However, this alone is not, and should not be, the sole driver for practitioners engaging with research; research should come from practitioners' passion to provide the best service to, and gain the best outcomes for, their clients. Practitioners have opportunities to engage with evidence-based practice to inform their clinical work as well as participate in gathering practice-based evidence, which together form a holistic approach to developing practice. In doing so, therapists can be more confident of making a difference with clients who are at the centre of counselling, and in contributing to wider clinical work.

SUGGESTED FURTHER READING

Aveyard, H and Sharp, P (2012) *A Beginner's Guide to Evidence-based Practice in Health and Social Care.* Milton Keynes: Open University Press.

An excellent text that covers multiple elements of evidence-based practice. Although aimed at health and social care students, much of the information is relevant and useful for counsellors and psychotherapists wanting to know more about evidence-based practice.

Barkham, M, Hardy, GE and Mellor-Clark, J (2010) *Developing and Delivering Practice-based Evidence: A guide for the psychological therapies.* West Sussex: Wiley Blackwell.

An accessible read for practitioners.

CHAPTER 4

Switching on your curiosity: developing research ideas

Graham Bright and Gill Harrison

CORE KNOWLEDGE

By the end of this chapter, you will be able to:

- identify and rationalise a manageable research topic;
- formulate an appropriate question;
- position yourself reflexively within the chosen study.

Research questions both inform and are informed by research conceptualisation, and articulate the essence of what research is about. They influence the epistemological stance that the researcher adopts (see Chapter 5), the data that is collected and how the data is analysed. The formulation of an appropriate research question is therefore fundamental to the direction and success of any project (Alvesson and Sandberg, 2013). Effective question construction enables the researcher to articulate and maintain a clear and focused framework, and helps the research to be appropriately boundaried (Savin-Baden and Major, 2013). Yet, so often, practitioner-researchers find question-framing illusive and slippery. Research questions can therefore take time to construct and articulate, and may require several iterative cycles in order to be rendered 'perfect'. A lack of clarity at this stage, however, is magnified later and often leads to ongoing confusion and disorientation as the project progresses. Research questions drive the direction and shape of what follows, and time spent at this juncture in refining them is a wise investment.

The answerability of a research question is integral to research design. Researchers must consider whether it is possible to develop reasonable responses to the questions they set, given potential constraints in finance and time. Many novice researchers make the fundamental error of posing grand questions that could easily encompass a professional researcher's entire career, rather than framing a question that can be attainably answered within the limitations of undergraduate or Master's level study. Research questions ought therefore to be clear, succinct and manageable.

Some literature in the area of research formation suggests particular strategies for developing appropriately framed questions. In line with the pursuit of originality, Alvesson and Sandberg (2013) argue that researchers should identify potential knowledge gaps that might be exploited through extensive reviews of subject literature. Such an argument is founded in particular disciplines and professional frameworks (in this instance social science and management studies) and draws upon a rationale that research should generate path-breaking theoretical concepts. Perhaps the idea of 'problematising' (challenging assumptions in the extant literature), also posited by Alvesson and Sandberg, is better aligned with therapists' professional values concerning applied research. This, however, highlights that the development of research questions is driven and shaped by a range of factors, including the motivation, beliefs and personal and professional values of the researcher. These drivers fundamentally fashion the types of questions that researchers ask, and the approaches to research that are pursued.

While we recognise that some students may find the ideas outlined above helpful, and acknowledge the value of utilising some of the suggested processes, we would argue that their application can in some instances be overly mechanistic and counter-intuitive to counselling students who are concerned with particular personal and professional ways of knowing that are founded in therapeutic thinking. The conscientisation of therapeutic material sometimes happens in apparently sudden light-bulb moments of realisation, and sometimes through the slow burning of unconscious materials and meanings that gradually slot into place in a way that gives crystallised panoramic understanding. In the same way, research questions are formed by the synthesis of different experiences at some level of our awareness, bubbling up into our consciousness; sometimes this is an instantaneous experience, sometimes a gradual jigsaw. Flick argues that the origins of research questions lie *in the researchers' personal biographies [and] social contexts* (2010, p98). The ways in which our narratives are historicised on personal, familial, social, professional, institutional and political levels are therefore fundamental to research formation. Such analysis makes clear that our experiences and the research questions that arise from them do not evolve in a vacuum. As Ransome notes:

> *a key aspect of the question-forming and question-asking process is to remain aware of the multi-dimensional nature of the social reality about which the researcher is asking questions.*
>
> (2013, p69)

Research questions, like interventions in the therapeutic system, are gateways to knowledge (Flick, 2010); both have the capacity to bring into conscious awareness that which is 'unknown'. Both are concerned with elucidating human meaning, experience and motivation. Devereux (1967) seminally argued that research questions in psychological disciplines arise from the researcher's unconscious processes. In this way, Etherington reflects that *the choice of research topic often has personal significance for the researcher, whether conscious or unconscious* . . . (2006, pp49–50). Moreover, Denscombe posits that researchers pay insufficient *attention to explaining what exactly motivated the investigation and what precisely they were trying to find out* (2010, pp7–8). These ideas present both a clear challenge and a point of access to counselling practitioner-researchers who are continually engaged in the quest for meaning in their therapeutic work.

It may be helpful at this point to consider the etymology of some of the present ideas. 'Question' has as its root word 'quest', which derives from the Latin *quaerere* – to ask or seek. The idea of seeking is integral to research, which involves us in exploring and seeking out potential answers. Etymologically, this relates to the Greek *heuriskein*, a root of 'eureka' (I have found it). *Heuriskein* also gives us 'heuristic', a word associated with Clark Moustakas' (1990) foundational model of deep intrapersonal inquiry, which places the researcher at the centre of the search for knowledge and insight. While readers may not wish to pursue an entire research project utilising a heuristic methodology, we would argue that its particular ontology is well aligned with the values of counselling and psychotherapy, and its initial stages offer rich potential to facilitate the generation of questions that are of real meaning and value to practitioner-researchers in the field.

Moustakas posited:

> *All heuristic inquiry begins with the internal search to discover with an encompassing puzzlement, a passionate desire to know, a devotion and commitment to pursue a question that is strongly connected to one's own identity and selfhood. The awakening of such a question comes through an inward clearing, and an intentional readiness and determination to discover a fundamental truth regarding the meaning and essence of one's own experience and that of others.*
>
> (1990, p40)

Some students approach research with a clearly formulated question in mind; for others there is awareness of a vague topic or theme that requires pinpointing and reworking into a researchable question, while a third category presents without a discernible idea of what they want to do. Research questions often come out of practice and experience. We may find our curiosity is stimulated by a particular client issue, client group or theoretical perspective; we may be enthused by reading or have opinions about new policies or procedures introduced by our funding agents. Tapping into the essence of the topic or question is of central importance; heuristic question-forming engages the researcher in a process of self-dialogue in order to reach a multifaceted understanding of the research kernel and the entirety of its meaning as it is understood in all levels of consciousness.

Heuristic research, therefore, connects the multifacetedness of human inquisitiveness in synthesising that which can be deeply known cognitively, affectively, bodily and spiritually. Heuristic question-framing fosters deep wonderment and absorption in mystery; it allows untapped human meaning to be excavated, enabling us to embrace the unknown, thereby facilitating the *internal search of researchers in their attempts to explore, collect and interpret data holistically* (Kenny, 2012, p6). In these ways, the researcher embodies the research question; indeed, he or she often comes to live, breathe, eat and dream about it. Research is a challenge; students should be passionate about their questions in order that they sustain them through the long hours of study. Here, McLeod notes that: *The assumption that underpins heuristic research is that the passionate involvement of the researcher will enable a depth of sustained examination of a topic* . . . (2011b, p206). Heuristic question-framing enables passionate questions to be generated, because the question, like volcanic lava, comes from the depths of the researcher's tacit, intrinsic experience.

Moustakas wrote that . . . *heuristic research involves self-search, self-dialogue and self-discovery; the research question and the methodology flow out of inner awareness, meaning and inspiration* (1990, p11). It promotes congruent intuitive knowing about the shape, feel, size and colour of phenomena, and wonderment about the very essence of the 'topic' that fosters a union or oneness between the researcher and the research phenomenon.

In this way, Moustakas argued:

> *Within each researcher exists a topic, theme, problem, or question that represents the critical interest and area of search. The task of the initial engagement is to discover an intense interest, a passionate concern that calls out to the researcher, one that holds important social meanings and personal, compelling implications. The initial engagement invites self-dialogue, an inner search to discover the topic and question* . . . *[Moustakas encouraged his readers to]: enter into dialogue with the phenomenon, allowing the phenomenon to speak directly to one's own experience, to be questioned by it.*
>
> (ibid., pp27/16)

Such an idea is reminiscent of our interactions with ourselves or with our clients; we seek to know self and Others, and the essence of experience through the richness of insight and transcendence. It reminds us too of 'empty-chair' work in Gestalt therapy, where the client searches for insight or completeness from an invisible or missing Other.

ACTIVITY 4.1

- Place something that represents the research topic or the shape of the emergent phenomenon in an empty chair. Either alone, or with the help of a peer, dialogue with the phenomenon. Let it speak to you.
- Be aware of your thoughts and sensations; what ideas, feelings and 'essences' begin to evolve?

As we have noted, research questions often arise out of practitioners' inquisitiveness concerning phenomena experienced somewhere in the therapeutic system. Whether this concerns practice or outcomes with specific client groups, relational processes in therapy, client experience of counselling, the efficacy of counsellor training (McLeod et al., 2010), or something else entirely, thematic or topical ideas must be distilled into manageable questions to give the research definition and focus.

In this way, McLeod posits:

> A research **topic** usually refers to a broad area of interest, within which many questions can be asked. A research question is like a searchlight that illuminates parts of this area of interest, or like a tool for dissecting it or digging into it.
>
> (1999, p46; emphasis in original)

The task here is for the researcher to refine his or her thinking and begin to pinpoint the question that might be asked. Developing a research rationale helps the researcher to make his or her intentions and motivations more explicit, giving greater focus to the task; it generates a conceptual framework that enables the purpose and aims of the research to become more overtly articulated, thereby fostering clarity.

Engaging in these processes allows the overarching research question (and subsidiary questions) to take on a more discernible form (see Figure 4.1). The key here is to support constructive or congruent alignment between different conceptual elements in order to ensure that the research is appropriately rationalised. This process in turn informs the choice of methodology and data collection and analysis methods.

In this way, White argues:

> Moving from topics to aims and objectives can be a useful step towards formulating research questions. Aims and objectives provide more direction than do topics and can help you start thinking about exactly what you

want to achieve in your study. While the aims and objectives of a study tend to be less specific than research questions they are more useful than topics or areas of interest for directing an investigation. Unlike topics, they identify the outcomes (or 'goals') that are desired and point to the kind of questions that would need to be asked in order to achieve these outcomes.

(2009, pp33–4)

Activities 4.2 and 4.3 will help you apply these ideas.

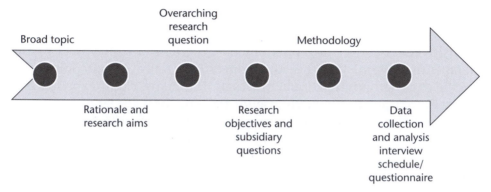

Figure 4.1: Rationalising research

ACTIVITY 4.2

Spend a few moments thinking about your current practice. You might think about the clients you are working with, the issues they bring, the relationship you have with different clients or perhaps the way in which the agency you work/volunteer for structures the number of sessions available and the assessment and review methods used.

• What are the areas that hold the most interest for you now?
• Make a list of all of the areas of interest. Rank them in order of curiosity.

From this activity, it may be possible to make interconnections between the ideas or topics that might be researched.

• What connections can you make? Diagramming these might be of help.

Example – Sarah

Statement
What are the significant activities or events that contribute to personal development in professional counsellor training?

Rationale
During my counsellor training I was aware of significant differences between students in relation to their personal development. Some of my peers, whilst having the academic ability to pass written assessments, seemed to be lacking in personal development, yet they seemed on track to pass their qualification and would then be 'out there' counselling vulnerable clients. It concerned me that personal development seemed such a difficult area to measure. I am interested in looking at personal development in counsellor training, and what is 'sufficient' personal development.

Looking at the statement (which will be refined into the research question), do you think that the rationale and the statement match?

The statement is asking about the activities or events that contribute to personal development, yet the rationale is suggesting there is a doubt about the sufficiency of personal development in some of Sarah's peers. Is she suggesting that the personal development assessment criteria were not robust enough to measure sufficiency in students' level of personal development? Is she qualified to comment on this? What unconscious processes might be going on for Sarah?

Let us imagine that Sarah had written her rationale as follows:

Rationale

During my counsellor training I was aware that many unexpected activities and events contributed to my personal development. I expected personal development to come out of the experiential group and my own personal therapy; however, I was surprised to find out that so many other things contributed to my growing self-awareness. I am interested to ask other newly qualified counsellors about their training to see if personal development can come from a wider range of activities and events.

Does this match the research question expressed above?

Congruent alignment of rationale and research question often takes time to finesse, but its importance cannot be overstated; it also affords researchers space to examine their own beliefs and motivations concerning their research topics and emerging questions, and to consider how they might position themselves reflexively within the research. In this way, the researcher provides a rationalised conceptual framework or matrix (see Figure 4.2), which they should continually revisit in order to ensure the research retains appropriate direction and scope (Hennink et al., 2011). The research framework must also take account of potential audiences, of which McLeod suggests there are principally five: . . . *the researcher, other counsellors, managers and policy makers, the general public and other researchers* (2007b, p24); these combined factors play a part in the type of question the researcher may wish to ask.

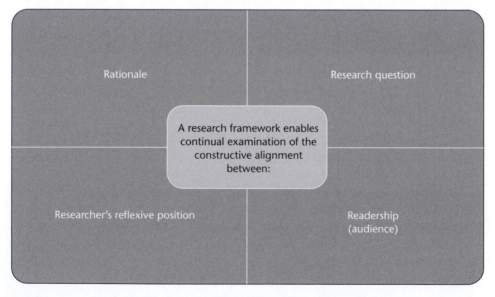

Figure 4.2: Rationalised conceptual framework

Case study 4.1

Dorothy worked for a voluntary sector counselling agency in the northeast of England, which served both male and female survivors of sexual abuse. Staff were coming under increasing pressure from funding organisations to work with victims who were also perpetrators of sexual abuse. Dorothy was concerned that offering such a service, within the same premises, could be detrimental to clients, staff and volunteers and from this developed her research question:

'How might allowing access to counselling for survivors of sexual abuse, who are also perpetrators, impact on the service provided by (agency name)?'

The aim of this project was to explore whether working with survivors of sexual abuse, who were also perpetrators of abuse, would impact on a specific voluntary sector agency working with both men and women. Beneath this main research questions were further objectives:

- to consider how changing agency policy might impact on staff (both paid and voluntary);
- to consider how it might impact on clients;
- to examine how it might impact on resources.

In this case, the topic was of interest to the researcher herself, other counsellors within the agency, managers and policy makers, as well as the general public accessing the service. The study led to the decision that the agency would not offer counselling support for victims who were also perpetrators within the same venue. In addition, Dorothy went on to present her research findings in a workshop at a regional research conference.

ACTIVITY 4.4

Consider the following questions.

- What or who is your intended research audience?
- How might this influence the development of your research question?

DIFFERENT TYPES OF QUESTIONS

McLeod et al. (2010, p22) suggest two principal question types that researchers ask: exploratory and confirmatory. Exploratory questions tend to be associated with description of a phenomenon, while confirmatory questions test hypotheses regarding a given phenomenon that has undergone some form of previous investigation. Hypotheses make predictions concerning research phenomena, often using measurable variables. The advantage of this type of research question or proposition is its capacity to generate specific focus (Barker et al., 2002). Hypothesis testing is located in the positivistic tradition of science-based inquiry, which seeks to apply rigorous scientific methodology to research investigation, including examination of the social world. Denscombe argues: *Hypotheses and propositions are suited to those styles of research which are involved with prediction of the results and with explaining the cause of phenomena* (2010, p16). White notes: *Because a hypothesis is simply a predicted answer to a research question it is important to be clear about the question you are asking as well as the answer you expect* (2009, p53). For example, a researcher's hypothesis might read: 'Proportionally fewer people who live in socially and economically disadvantaged areas (using the Indices of Multiple Deprivation, 2010 (HM Government, 2010)) access therapy than those living in non-disadvantaged areas.'

Such a statement, however, must also be framed as a question, and might read: 'Do proportionally fewer people who live in socially and economically disadvantaged areas (using the Indices of Multiple Deprivation, 2010) access therapy than those living in non-disadvantaged areas?' Clearly, such a question requires further definition. This data set lists some 32,482 Lower Layer Super Output Areas (LSOAs); these are relatively small geographical areas with a given number of people in each. In this instance, clear and rationalised justification that takes account of wider definitions of 'disadvantage' needs to be considered in order to validate which LSOAs fit within each category (disadvantaged and non-disadvantaged).

The type of question asked therefore both influences and is influenced by epistemological ideas. As McLeod notes: *Qualitative research tends to be based around open-ended, 'discovery-orientated' questions . . . A quantitative research study, by contrast, needs to be much more precisely defined* (1999, p48).

Figure 4.3 maps aspects of the 'question terrain'.

Figure 4.3: The 'question terrain'
(after Denscombe, 2010; McLeod et al., 2010)

ACTIVITY 4.5

Researchers must therefore ask themselves 'What type of answers am I looking for?' The response to this question will determine the type of question that should be asked.

Consider the following questions.

- What kind of answers are you seeking?
- In which way are your questions most likely to be answered?
- What methods would you use to achieve this?
- Are there any potential ethical issues that arise here?

Relate your responses to these questions to the research framework/matrix outlined in Figure 4.2.

Case study 4.2

In my (Graham's) own research (Bright, 2011), I was interested in how children and young people understood and experienced the phenomenon of resilience. My own professional practice left me eager to discover how counselling in school contexts might enable resilience to be built among cohorts who experience particular forms of (primarily economic and social) 'disadvantage'. The exploratory and experiential nature of the topic led to the development of a research question that was, in retrospect, too closed and perhaps did not truly reflect the essence of its intentions. Despite this, the research succeeded in getting close to the essence of the phenomenon as experienced by my participants, as the sub-questions and those that formed my interview schedule better reflected what I wanted to know. However, with hindsight, better constructive alignment would have enabled me not only to 'get there more quickly', but perhaps also to gain 'richer' results. My research question perhaps therefore ought to have been: 'How do children and young people experience the potential development of resilience in the context of school counselling?' This question better expresses what I wanted to know and how I wanted to know it. It is exploratory and concerned with understanding and attempting to become phenomenologically close to pupil-contributors' personal understandings of resilience.

Ideas pertaining to participant experience, perceptions, views and questions (or statements) that are framed in a process-orientated fashion, for example, 'Towards a lived understanding of transcendence in counselling in psychotherapy: a therapist's view' or 'Towards a lived understanding of sexual transference in the therapeutic system', reflect an open-ended, exploratory and phenomenological ideal (Smith et al., 2009), while 'Is CBT more effective than psychodynamic therapies in the treatment of depressed adolescents?' is certainly more direct, closed and quantitatively bounded. Neither question type is 'right or wrong', but informed (as we shall see in Chapters 5 and 8) by different values and assumptions. Each drives a different road to knowing, and different vehicles to get there.

We move again to consider the structure of research inquiry. The capacity to break down the overarching research question into constituent elements in order to articulate the objectives of the research is of real importance; this process enables the questions that form the basis of an interview schedule (in the case of qualitative inquiry) to emerge. Some researchers of course construct their main question by interlinking objectives; our advice is that researchers should, where possible, refrain from this approach and develop the overarching question in the first instance in order to cultivate and better maintain constructive alignment in the work. It is far easier to amend an interview schedule or even an objective than shift the entire focus of the principal question. In this way, a researcher whose *topic* concerns the development of counsellors' professional identities might pose the following research question: 'How does the first year of post-qualifying practice shape counsellors' perceptions of professional selves?' From this question, the researcher needs to articulate in more detail what he or she wants the research to reveal. These objectives give rise to subsidiary questions, which, dependent on the methodology adopted, might form the basis of an interview schedule. Table 4.1 provides a worked example that utilises the above question.

There are some points to note from Table 4.1. First, good qualitative research should enable an exploratory understanding of phenomena from the perspective of the teller. Questions therefore ought to be open. Second, an overarching question should, in order to maintain the manageability of the project, generate no more than three or four objectives, which might be further broken down into sub-questions to form the basis of an interview schedule. Where more objectives emerge, the researcher should prioritise those that hold the deepest fascination, and note and retain the remainder for future research projects (White, 2009). Third, questions should be clear

Objective	Question
To find out how counsellors experience their first year of practice.	1. I wonder if you might tell me why and how you became a therapist? 2. Can you describe your experience of your first year of therapeutic practice?
To find out how the first year of practice shapes counsellors' professional identities.	3. Can you describe the key moments or processes that have shaped professional self-perception in your first year of practice? 4. How therefore do you feel your first year of practice has shaped your professional identity?
To find out how counsellors have experienced and reflexively co-constructed their relationships with their clinical supervisors and how this has informed their sense of professional self.	5. How have you experienced and 'used' your relationship with your supervisor? 6. Can you describe any changes you have experienced in the construction of that relationship in the last year? 7. How do you feel these changes have shaped your professional identity?

Table 4.1: Perceptions of professional selves

and not overly complex; they should ask participants about their thoughts, ideas and experiences by examining one thing at a time. Hennink et al. remind us that *The questions in an interview guide have to follow a logical order* (2011, p116). As with the example above (which draws on ideas from phenomenological and narrative research), interview schedules should be focused and move from the general to the specific. This allows the story to be understood in its context. Furthermore, it could be quite threatening for participants to be asked overly direct questions early in a research interview; thought therefore needs to be given to structuring the interview schedule to enable time for rapport between researcher and participant to be built. Research interviews have often been described as 'conversations with a purpose'; interview schedules should therefore act as frameworks to facilitatively guide rather than restrictively direct research interactions. Prompting questions ('Can you tell me more about that, please?') and probing questions ('What do you mean by "enlightening"?') are therefore legitimate interventions to enable clarity and deeper understanding.

CHAPTER SUMMARY

Therapists are used to asking questions; and, as we have noted, research, like therapy, engages the practitioner-researcher in the pursuit of knowledge and meaning. This chapter has sought to provide a practical framework that enables readers to generate manageable and constructively aligned questions while drawing on the heuristic methodologies of Clark Moustakas to argue that all research geneses lie somewhere within the researcher.

SUGGESTED FURTHER READING

Moustakas, C (1990) *Heuristic Research*. London: Sage.

This seminal text unpacks research as an intensely intrapersonal process through which transformational and transcendent questions and meanings are dialogically constructed.

White, P (2009) *Developing Research Questions*. Basingstoke: Palgrave Macmillan.

A practical and insightful text that helps student-researchers formulate effective questions.

CHAPTER 5

Making sense of 'ologies'

Graham Bright

CORE KNOWLEDGE

By the end of this chapter, you will be able to:

- explain philosophical ideas underpinning different research approaches;
- evaluate different types of knowledge;
- appraise a range of research methodologies used in counselling and psychotherapy;
- select methodologies that might be suitable for your own research project.

Picture the scene – it's 1987 and a well-known telecommunications company is launching a new series of adverts. Beattie Bellman is on the phone speaking with her disconsolate sixteen-year-old grandson Anthony, who has just failed all his exams except pottery and sociology. As she hears the word 'sociology' she famously exclaims: 'An ology! He gets an ology and says he's failed – you get an ology, you're a scientist!'

The 'ology' suffix is attached to different disciplines in the arts, medicine, the sciences and social sciences, and conjures up many different thoughts that might elicit different responses in readers. 'Ology' comes from the Greek 'logos' meaning 'study of': there is a range of 'ologies' contained within ideas about research that are important to grasp and apply; the first we shall consider is *epistemology* or the study of knowledge.

Epistemology as a branch of philosophy requires researchers to consider questions about the nature of reality and the types of knowledge deemed valid. Bager-Charleson notes that: *Epistemology asks questions about the bedrock and ultimate foundations of belief* (2010, p73). Langridge and Hagger-Johnson (2009) extend the importance of this by arguing that epistemology is concerned with how we understand, construct and validate our understanding of the world. At their core, epistemological positions require us to consider whether knowledge is created through scientific investigation, or through interpretations of the socially constructed world. Epistemology is therefore not only concerned about the nature of reality, or what reality is, but how we conceptualise and validate the ways in which our understanding of reality is reached (Denscombe, 2010). Bryman argues that *methods of social research are closely tied to different visions of how social reality should be studied* (2008, p4). Researchers then must consider the type of knowledge that is sought to ensure that the knowledge that is produced is *valid, useful and acceptable* (McLeod, 2007a, p178).

ACTIVITY 5.1

• Think about counselling. Produce a mind map about what you know about therapy and how you came to that knowledge.
• Work with a partner, share your ideas on what you have learned from this exercise and consider what other learning this generates.

From this activity, it is possible to reflect on different types of knowledge that have been developed and used to construct a wider body of knowledge on the relatively narrow subject of counselling. Perhaps in addition to other ideas you have generated, we can appreciate that knowledge about counselling comes from different sources, as illustrated in Figure 5.1.

Learning and knowledge about counselling therefore involves integration of different types of knowledge, both cognitive and embodied, from which

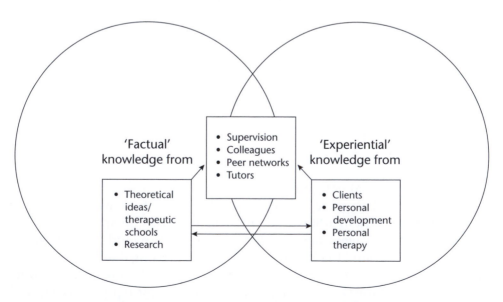

Figure 5.1: Knowledge bases in counselling

new and reflexive forms of knowing continue to grow. Both 'factual' and 'experiential' knowledge bases are of value in the pursuit of developing counselling as a profession; however, as we will note, different episte-mological positions value these in different ways.

One of the great thinkers of our time is the philosopher Edward de Bono. In his book *Six Thinking Hats* de Bono (1999) introduces his idea of different ways of approaching and thinking about concepts, ideas and experiences. He notes that *the main difficulty of thinking is confusion. We try to do too much at once. Emotions, information, logic, hope and creativity all crowd in on us* (ibid., pxi). He contends that we need to put on different 'thinking hats' at different times in order to create appropriate, rounded and integrated approaches to developing knowledge, understanding and problem solving: a capacity that is essential in helping researchers utilise different thinking skills during different elements of the research process.

Hat	Purpose and function in thinking
White	Objective, factual forms of knowledge.
Red	Emotional and intuitive ways of knowing.
Black	Helps us think in an evaluatory fashion – to stand back and think critically about the strengths and weaknesses in an idea or approach.
Yellow	Hopeful and positive ways of thinking.
Green	A way of thinking that encourages space for creativity.
Blue	Organises thinking processes, giving precedence to the other hats where each is appropriate. The Blue Hat asks us to consider what hat is appropriate to wear.

Table 5.1: De Bono's *Six Thinking Hats* (after de Bono (1999))

POSITIVISM

We turn our attention here to the first of the epistemological paradigms we will explore – positivism. Positivism philosophically holds the 'White Hat' position that the world and social reality are scientifically constructed and should be scientifically interrogated. As such, prediction, testable hypothe-ses and measurement in (preferably) controlled environments, which seek to eliminate and understand active ingredients in scientific experiments, are of real importance to the positivist worldview. Positivists therefore hold a 'realist' position and *regard the social world as something that exists 'out there'* (Denscombe, 2010, p119). Hennink et al. argue that:

> *within positivism, there is an emphasis on objective measurement of* **social** *issues, where it is assumed that reality consists of* **facts** *and that researchers can observe and measure reality in an* **objective** *way* . . .

> (2011, p14; emphasis added)

According to the positivist worldview, therefore, all matter including social and therapeutic 'matter' can and should be tested in a rigorous, scientific manner.

Positivistic thinking can be traced back to the Ancient Greek philosophers; however, it becomes increasingly connected to modern-day thinking through the work of the French philosopher and sociologist Auguste Comte (1798–1857). Comte was a product of the Enlightenment, an eighteenth-century philosophical movement, which stood for the progression of society through scientific reasoning over superstition and unfounded belief.

The Enlightenment was a time of great advancement, where beliefs held in orthodoxy (the accepted view) were philosophically scrutinised through scientific investigation. Comte's promotion of the positivist philosophy led to *a general doctrine of positivism which held that all genuine knowledge is based on sense experience and can be advanced only by means of observation and experiment* (Cohen et al., 2007, p9). Positivism therefore holds the position that, just as all matter in the physical sciences can be scientifically interrogated in a highly objective manner, so too can the social world as embodied in human experience. These concepts, as you will note, link to ideas on evidence-based practice, as forms of scientific and medical investigation, that have been developed in Chapter 3. Counselling too has witnessed the increased demand for evidence-based practice through rigorous, science-based inquiry, most notably randomised controlled trials (RCTs), which Dallos and Vetere (2005, p78) contend are the 'gold standard' of positivistic research. RCTs are utilised in clinical trials in the medical field to test the efficacy of treatment interventions. Participants from a usually large sample are randomly assigned to different 'conditions', which might include no intervention (also known as a control group), placebic intervention and treatment intervention(s), in order to test the effectiveness of the drug being trialled. Results are measured against pre-ordained baselines and scientific conclusions drawn about the intervention's efficacy.

In counselling, RCTs are used to provide evidence of the effectiveness of specific interventions using predetermined numerical baselines. Timulak

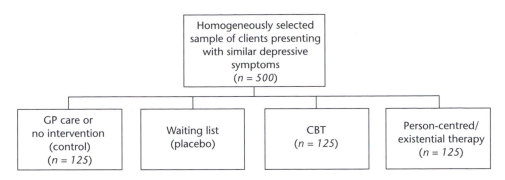

Figure 5.2: Example of a randomised controlled trial

argues that RCTs are used to capture the *causal links in therapy* (2008, p44). In the example in Figure 5.2, a homogeneous sample are asked to scale their presenting depressive symptoms from which baseline data is generated (the sample might be more fully controlled according to a further range of factors including age and gender etc.). The cohort is randomly allocated to a given number of interventions from which comparative results are generated. The standard control group is classically defined as no intervention; however, ethical issues can ensue dependent on what factors are being 'tested'. Therefore, as a result in counselling RCTs, the standard control protocol is often to place 'control' participants on a waiting list. It should be noted, however, that some research suggests that control clients can show some improvement by anticipating that they will be helped, and this needs to be appropriately factored into the research results (Cooper, 2008). Symptoms are rescaled post-intervention and conclusions drawn about the efficacy of interventions in comparison to control and placebo groups.

There has been (and continues to be) much discussion in the counselling profession about the place and indeed the ethics of applying such approaches to counselling and psychotherapy. The increasing availability of therapeutic services in the UK, including the National Health Service-sponsored Improving Access to Psychological Therapies (IAPT), has been grounded in evidenced-based approaches. Particular therapeutic schools, most notably cognitive behavioural therapy (CBT) (which is IAPT's primary therapeutic approach), have embraced positivistic research. This has enabled the generation of a considerable evidence base, which continues to justify the place of CBT within government-funded initiatives such as IAPT. Such trail-blazing has challenged the wider psychotherapeutic community, and led to significant amounts of research, including comparative meta-analyses of different therapeutic approaches (see Cooper, 2008; Timulak, 2008; Timulak and Creaner, 2010), much of which evidences the essential efficacious value of comparative therapeutic modalities. Many therapists, however, irrespective of modality, would to a greater or lesser degree describe their work as being concerned with the essence of human experience. This has led to some reluctance to merely condense therapeutic work to a scientifically reductionist position of inputs and outputs that might be equated to clients with 'X symptoms' engage with 'Y' therapy with 'Z' outcomes. Some writers, such as House et al. (2011) and Elliott and Freire (2010), have vehemently argued that the profession should reject such a reductionist worldview, which in their view runs contrary to the very essence of counselling, while others, such as Cooper (2011), have argued that the therapeutic world should pragmatically embrace RCTs in order to produce the type of research that is both required by funders and supports clinical excellence in the profession. Others still, including McArthur (2011), have joined the debate to offer their own experiences of RCTs. McArthur highlights ways in which RCTs can be used not only as a means of producing objective and scientifically rigorous data, but also as a catalyst for further qualitative inquiry, which 'drills down' beyond numbers, to elucidate more of the participants' experiences of therapy.

RCTs can by their very nature be highly time-consuming, and require considerable numbers of participants in order that their results be considered valid. Given, too, that ethical approval for RCTs can sometimes be difficult to attain, it would be unlikely that many counselling students on undergraduate and Master's programmes would consider pursuing such a research project. This, however, is not to detract from the growing value that many both within and external to the profession place on RCTs in developing powerful empirical evidence bases for the efficacy of therapeutic work.

Many therapists do, however, regularly use numbers to help evaluate practice. Tools, including Clinical Outcomes in Routine Evaluation (CORE – www.coreims.co.uk), Helpful Aspects of Therapy (HAT) forms (Elliott, 1993) and the Rickter Scale (Hutchinson and Stead, 1993), enable counsellors to numerically capture therapeutic change both in and at the end of therapy for individual clients. Data of this nature can then be collated by individual therapists and across organisations to construct evidence on the helpfulness of therapeutic work, both generally and according to specific criteria (age, gender, presenting issue etc.). Quantitative research, therefore, is of real value in enabling researchers to create headline, 'big picture' evidence, which can begin to form the basis of generalisable, nomothetic (universal) ideas about the effectiveness of therapy.

ACTIVITY 5.2

Reflect on, record and discuss with others your thoughts on the different perspectives raised regarding positivistic forms of research within counselling and psychotherapy.

- What are the issues that are raised for you?
- How might this impact your personal views on your own research?
- How might you consider incorporating quantitative approaches within your research?

ANTI-POSITIVISM

We turn our attention now to the other epistemological position: anti-positivism. You may see anti-positivism referred to as post-positivism and interpretivism within literature. Anti-positivism might be thought of as a family of methodological ideas and approaches associated with 'Red and Green Hat thinking', which we will begin to examine here. Interpretivism, as Timulak (2008, p55) notes, has witnessed a 'huge development' in recent years. Interpretivists hold the position that reality is constructed in and through people's experiences of the world, and that humans as sense-making creatures (Langdridge, 2007) construct that meaning introspectively and through various forms of 'dialogue' with others. Whereas we might think of positivism as being concerned with the construction of more absolute forms of 'truth' through scientific systems of inquiry in order to produce absolute and transferable forms of knowledge, interpretivism is concerned with the construction of localised or ideographic knowledge (McLeod, 2007a; Bager-Charleson, 2010; Denscombe, 2010), in generating rich data that emphasises and conveys human experience and meaning. The movement from the modern era, which was characterised by a greater sense of uniformity between people, to the postmodern period (since the Second World War), in which people increasingly and reflexively construct their own life-biographies with less deference to particular social systems, has heightened researchers' interest in different forms of narrative research. As Flick notes: *Rapid social change and the resulting diversification of life worlds are increasingly confronting social researchers with new social contexts and perspectives* (2010, p12). Therefore, whereas positivism is concerned with the construction of 'a single reality', interpretivism enables the discovery of different, multiple realities (ibid.; see also Denscombe, 2008, 2010).

ACTIVITY 5.3

Work with a partner. Briefly (10–15 minutes) interview each other about significant life events that have led you both to train as therapists.

- What is unique about both stories? What similarities are there? What thoughts and feelings do you become aware of?

By reflecting on this relatively ad hoc 'interview' experience, it might become noticeable that aspects of your partner's experience resonate particularly with your own, while other parts you might feel no personal connection with other than your own empathic understanding of their experience. Some parts of your partner's story might in some way mingle with your own in the same way that a client's story might intertwine with the therapist's past or present personal narrative. There are rich stories to be experienced, understood and retold, and here we begin to find our understanding of other 'ologies'.

Whereas *ontology* is concerned with our own particular view of reality, *axiology* examines ethical and value-based assumptions that are held as important to individuals. Ontological and axiological positions often develop from the convergence of different experiences that shape our personal understanding and experiencing of something. As such, qualitative research is a heuristic process, germinating within and emanating from the researcher (Moustakas, 1990). It is the researcher who becomes the primary research instrument, and as such the researcher must engage in listening to him- or herself *and* his or her participants in order to enhance the reflexive processes involved in qualitative inquiry (Pezalla et al., 2012). Ontological and axiological loci can therefore be powerful sources of initial research ideas, and produce rich interactions between the researcher and the research process. However, they can also be the seat of personal bias, and as such should be explored, expressed and reflexively examined as part of research practice.

If we were to take the example of the reason people become therapists in Activity 5.3, we might hold the position because it is our own (or perhaps others' whom we know) experience that people are motivated towards becoming therapists because of challenging personal experiences in their past; here our approach to research becomes impacted by this or other similarly held beliefs. As such the process of effective qualitative research requires that we interrogate ourselves with the help of others in order to elucidate these particular positions and beliefs that are (as so often within the therapeutic process) awaiting discovery. In discerning our own position within the research we are able to *bracket off* (Smith et al., 2009, p99) our assumptions in order to enable the research to travel in a more objective direction. Qualitative research can be rewarding yet demanding, especially for therapists who are concerned with their own personal and professional journey (Adams, 2012; Bager-Charleson, 2012). The support of peers, support networks, and clinical and academic supervisors is therefore essential to the exploratory process, which so often ensues in qualitative research in counselling, and which for many becomes in part at least a process of self-inquiry. It is clear, therefore, that the qualitative researcher is situated within, rather than removed from, the process of the research; and, as such, research becomes a network of relationships between the researcher, the research, research participants, peers and the self. Therapy is about relationships, and many counselling students find themselves drawn to qualitative research as a means of co-creating knowledge in a process that runs parallel to the therapeutic endeavour itself (Finlay and Evans, 2009; Reason and Riley, 2009).

Here, high degrees of reflexivity are required in order to create the conditions for a dynamic and continually recursive relationship between the researcher and the research (Pezalla et al., 2012). As Finlay and Evans note: *More than owning and sharing ourselves, we need to examine reflexively how our own conscious and unconscious selves may be impacting upon the research process and outcomes* (2009, p37). Researchers are therefore required in qualitative work to give themselves to a *dynamic process of interaction* (Etherington, 2004, p32) between themselves, their participants, the subject literature and the intricacies of the overall research process.

ACTIVITY 5.4

You may by now have some initial ideas about the subject(s) you wish to explore in a research project. If you have not done so already, write these down.

- Without thinking too deeply about it, brainstorm all the ideas you have around that subject.
- Reflect for yourself and with others about the beliefs (ontology) and values (axiology) you hold about that subject. How, for example, are these ideas and beliefs informed by therapeutic theory and practice?

Case study 5.1

Erica was a mature student who had worked for many years in nursing. After finishing her Foundation Degree in Counselling, she decided to go on to study for a BA Honours (Top-up) award. Erica had worked with bereaved clients in a local hospice for a few years and wanted to focus the research for her dissertation on bereavement counselling. Coming from a medical background, which values evidence-based practice, she appeared to want to 'disprove' the effectiveness of counselling bereaved clients. The influence of such a positivist position seemed to clash with the qualitative methodology she adopted, and the process of engaging with research, particularly in the early stages, was challenging as a result. The research question she eventually framed was: 'How bereavement counselling enhances the bereavement process, or is time the great healer?' Through the process of undertaking the research and with the support of peers and tutors, Erica eventually came to a very personal realisation. Prior to becoming a counsellor, her father had passed away. Erica's and her siblings' way of dealing with this at the time was not to talk about their feelings. None of her family, including Erica's mum, accessed any form of bereavement counselling or support, and in order to manage her own responses to her loss, she would attempt to close her mum down when the subject of her father was raised. Erica's mum died within a year of her dad. Erica came to the awareness that her research question was not only about the experience of clients, it was a question that was rooted in her own unconscious experience: if mum had had counselling, might she have lived? This growing awareness of the locus of the research question enabled Erica to go on an unexpected, challenging, but ultimately cathartic, personal journey that helped her to reconcile aspects of her own past. This new awareness was not only personally enriching for Erica, it enabled her to deal with the research subject reflexively and with growing objectivity as she interviewed fellow counsellors about their experiences of working with bereaved clients.

ACTIVITY 5.5

In considering the case study above, it is clear that qualitative research can be a lonely and personally demanding, but nonetheless enriching experience; it becomes a space for personal development, and a place to 'gather selves' (Etherington, 2001). Bager-Charleson reflects that *our own involvement [in research] means that we more often than not will learn something new about ourselves as part of the research process* (2012, p110).

Wenger (2008) locates a range of life practices (in which we might include research) as 'communities of practice'. Very often the support of others, including fellow students, can provide the reciprocal spaces and nourishing lifelines that are needed at various points in the research process.

- Write down the different individuals and networks you might be able to draw on for support and those who may provide you with a 'sounding board'. How could you foster these relationships for this purpose?

QUALITATIVE METHODOLOGIES

We are able to think about qualitative methodologies as a family of ideas. As with most families, there are some shared resemblant characteristics that sit alongside both sibling rivalry and cooperative endeavour. We attempt here to *introduce* and explore aspects of different siblings' unique personalities; however, it should also be noted that qualitative research methodologies are required to be fit for purpose, and should be constructed and used in ways that are more evolutionary than explicitly defined, in order to be responsive and reflexive to what is happening in the research field. The researcher, as Smith et al. note, needs to *be creative in [the] application of these methods* (2009, p40). McLeod refers to this as *bricolage . . . [that which] require[s] the researcher to improvise and create his or her own techniques for collecting and analysing material* (2007b, p119).

Thematic analysis

Thematic analysis is probably the most accessible form of qualitative inquiry for novice researchers. It is, as Braun and Clarke (2006, p78) note, a 'foundational method' that provides an appropriate platform for beginner researchers to develop more complex approaches to qualitative research work. While it is true that most qualitative approaches have embedded within them the process of identifying themes that emerge from empirical data (and hence why some, including Ryan and Bernard (2000), have contended that thematic analysis is more of generic skill than a specific methodology in its own right), others including Boyatzis (1998), Braun and Clarke (2006) and Finlay (2011) have argued it as a justifiable research approach. Thematic analysis is epistemologically flexible. It is not bound to particular worldviews (e.g. *essentialism* – the reporting of essence of experience and meanings, or *constructionism* – how reality is understood in the light of particular socially constructed discourses, e.g. Foucault, Marx, Weber) as other qualitative approaches might be, enabling it to operate across or independently of particular philosophical positions (Braun and Clarke, 2006). Thematic analysis offers a particular resonance with psychodynamic approaches to therapy. Just as a psychodynamic counsellor is concerned with making interconnections between different aspects of his or her client's past and present:

> *The [research] analyst can start the thematic analysis by the open coding of data. This means building a set of themes by looking for patterns and meaning produced in the data, labelling and grouping them in connection with the theoretical framework of the research.*
>
> (Esin, 2011, p108)

However, it should be noted that thematic analysis, in contrast to other approaches, is concerned with raw research material rather than the nuances of how it is constituted or intonated. Thematic analysis is an approach that enables researchers to identify, code and cluster themes emerging from the research. It should be stated that the idea of 'emergence', as Finlay and Madill (2009) argue, is not one of passivity; rather, it requires researchers to be actively and iteratively engaged in seeking out meanings and connections. It requires them to interrogate the data, to ask themselves 'and what else, and what else, and what else . . .?'

As I write, the picture of a tanner comes to mind. The tanner takes raw material and treats it in such a way that it becomes fit and robust for a different purpose. He or she takes animal hide and processes it through a range of stages, some of which might be considered unpleasant, time-consuming or difficult, in order to produce a useful end product. In a similar way, qualitative data needs to be broken down and reconstituted in a way that remains true to its original meaning or construction while generating new perspectives on its possible significance or usefulness.

Many qualitative approaches seek to make thematic connections across an entire data set; however, thematic analysis is concerned with extracting themes within individual data items (e.g. an interview transcript or a journal excerpt), before examining thematic interconnections across data cohorts. Agreeing what constitutes a theme is a subjective endeavour, and good judgement from the researcher is therefore required (Braun and Clarke, 2006):

> *Ideally, there will be a number of instances of the theme across the data set, but more instances do not necessarily mean the theme itself is more crucial. As this is qualitative analysis, there is no hard-and-fast answer to the question of what proportion of your data set needs to display evidence of the theme for it to be considered a theme . . . A theme might be given considerable space in some data items, and little or none in others, or it might appear in relatively little of the data set . . . Furthermore, the 'keyness' of a theme is not necessarily dependent on quantifiable measures, but rather on whether it captures something important in relation to the overall research question.*
>
> (ibid., p82)

In their seminal paper Braun and Clarke (2006) suggest a six-stage iterative process to thematic analysis.

1. Active immersion in the data: listening to interviews; reading and rereading transcripts. Developing initial notes on noticeable patterns.
2. Generating initial codes. Considering and noting ideas of patterns that emerge across the data set, collating data that is significant to each code.
3. Organising the coded data into emergent themes, connecting the data in order to support the evolving themes.
4. Considering how the themes match the codes generated for each data item and across the entire data cohort.
5. Naming the themes and how they fit together in forming the overall research story.
6. Writing up the research by extracting engaging and persuasive excerpts that support the generated themes. These are synthesised with the reviewed literature in creating compelling arguments that accurately reflect participants' experiences and ideas.

Research participants' stories are at the centre of thematic analysis (Esin, 2011) and, as such, the themes that are developed and the research that is conveyed must remain grounded in the narratives generated by individuals and the cohort more broadly, and remain representative of the data. Thematic analysis is, as we have noted, an accessible qualitative approach that is worthy of primary consideration for novice researchers. It enables the elucidation of empirical data through the generation of thematic interconnections within a given data set in a flexible manner, which can be bound to or free from allegiance to particular philosophical paradigms.

DISCURSIVE METHODOLOGIES

Discursive methodologies are qualitative approaches to research that are concerned in different ways with the use of language. In counselling research, these methodologies consider the processes and use of language to both convey and co-construct meaning within and about therapy (McLeod, 2011b). Broadly speaking, there are three primary discursive methodologies that we will consider here: conversation analysis, discourse analysis and narrative analysis. It should be noted, however, that there are other derivative approaches associated with these three.

McLeod reflects that . . . *therapy is certainly an activity that relies heavily on the use of language* (ibid., p167). Language is the primary mechanism by which the client reveals, explores, processes and (re)constructs life and self in therapy. It is the narrator to the cine film of the client's life; a form of commentary by which the client gives voice to his or her life and experience, in order to enable the therapist to share in the client's lifeworld. Such conceptualisations have led to a growing interest in how language is used as a means of expressive interaction within therapy and as a mechanism to evaluate therapeutic processes. We might think of language as a tool with which to construct meaning, a brush with which to draw a picture, a musical instrument with which to evoke emotion or a catalyst with which to enact change. The nuances of verbal communication are not only about intention, but interpretation and the co-construction of understanding. Language used within and about therapy therefore provides a rich site within which to construct knowledge and understanding. Forms of discursive analysis often engage in analysing data generated through transcriptions of counselling sessions and may well relate to case study work (McLeod, 2010, 2011b), which many students are required to complete as part of their counselling training. Some of the processes involved in these forms of research might therefore be familiar.

Conversation analysis

Conversation analysis is concerned with the rigorous and critical examination of conversation within given institutional settings. Its key premise is to consider how conversation is constructed with particular reference to power dynamics. Conversational analysis is therefore a methodological approach that studies and develops theory about the conventions of interactions in particular settings, linking ideas to particular philosophical frameworks. One of its key proponents was the late French philosopher and academic Michel Foucault (1926–84), who developed particular ideas about human interaction based on power inequalities within social and organisational contexts (Schirato et al., 2012). Language and conversation convey, in often subtle ways, perceptions of our place in the world. Conversation becomes a site where identities are constructed, considered, challenged or re-enforced; it is a mechanism of enlightenment where we understand who we are, or at least how we are perceived in light of our relationships with others (Elliott, 2009). Conversation analysis holds the position that conversation is not merely about an interaction, it is the means by which social orders and *normative [contextual] expectations* (Drew, 2009, p135) are enacted. At its most basic level conversation becomes a contextualised dyadic process of repeated action and response, in which linguistic nuances of interplay between social actors can elucidate socially constructed positions. In considering the notion of institution, we might think about a range of different social organisations (e.g. government, the education system, religious groups, industry etc.) that hold sway within society. In conversation analysis the term 'institutions' can refer to a range of less formalised relationships that are theatres of social performance. In this way we can think of therapy as an institution, where particular dramas are played out (McLeod, 2011b).

Within therapy certain patterned linguistic conventions apply that are informed by a range of factors including therapeutic orientation. These patterns are different from other social interactions; in therapy clients may come to counselling in order to discuss particular issues, experiences or problems and are likely to be given considerable uninterrupted time and space to speak. This is different from other forms of interpersonal communication that are situated in medical, social, educational, professional or family contexts. Conversation analysis ethnomethodologically (research in highly localised contexts) examines the etiquette of interactions. It is concerned with the sequence of conversation, turn-taking, choice of language and ways in which conversations are *repaired* (Silverman, 2009, p212) when interruptions or misunderstandings occur. Data should be naturally generated (a recording of a therapy session is a prime example) and transcribed. Excerpts of the transcription are selected and examined in detail, with specific transcription symbols attached to each nuance of speech to indicate particular changes in intonation, use of paralanguage, speech patterns, volume, stresses, pitch etc. (see Drew, 2009). Given the level of considerable detail involved in this form of analysis, conversation analysis is not conducive to interrogating large swathes of data, therefore short extracts are selected for examination. Patterns, sequences and structures within interactions are examined and contextualised in order to examine ways in which actors engage with and manage their interactions.

This type of research is suitable for process-based case study approaches, or to compare a small number of individual cases. Conversation analysis is therefore a methodological approach that can give rise to critical insight and reflection, enabling the practitioner to consider in minutiae patterns of their interactions with clients and to reflect on this in light of particular theoretical frameworks. It has the capacity to illuminate ways in which therapy is constructed and enacted between client and therapist.

ACTIVITY 5.6

- Write down the different situations and contexts in which you engage in conversation.
- Record how these different situations influence roles and patterns in interactions.
- Compare what you notice with a fellow student.

Discourse analysis

Discourse analysis is viewed as having developed from conversation analysis, and although sharing particular characteristics has adopted alternative critical standpoints of its own. It is a methodological approach that has witnessed significant growth in recent years within the social sciences and within psychological study in particular (Willig, 2009). The notion of discourse is considered to be *a way of thinking, [which is] perhaps culturally or institutionally conditioned . . . [and] is legitimated by communities, often those with power* (Cohen et al., 2011, p574). Discourses tend to be oppositional, in that it is easier to identify rhetorically what they stand against, rather than stand for (McLeod, 2011b), therefore we might argue that discourse analysts seek to position themselves in comparison to alternative discourses in order to challenge intersubjective hegemony. Therefore, discourse analysis embeds something that is both subtly and overtly subversive and political. As an approach, discourse analysis is interested in language and how it is used in conveying, openly and covertly, meaning that reinforces and challenges intrapersonal, interpersonal and social constructs and norms within institutional and global contexts. Particular discourses therefore arise about the nature of society and how it is constructed. If we were to take, for example, therapy's relationship with wider society and class, and poverty in particular, we might see the discourses of certain texts challenging the therapeutic community about how it thinks and acts in relation to these subjects (see, for example, Proctor, 2006; Morrall, 2008). McLeod (2011b) argues that discourse analysis is more about particular dispositions, attitudes and stances as opposed to method. In these senses, therefore, we can assert that discourse analysis is closely aligned with *critical theory*, which posits an overtly radical and emancipatory research stance that opposes prevailing, accepted social norms that leave different forms of disadvantage and oppression unchallenged. The idea of positioning within discourse analysis is integral; research can create critical dialogue when diametric positions are examined. In counselling research, for example, discourse analysis can be utilised in single or multiple case study work to construct particular arguments about client experience of therapeutic change around given presenting issues, or the client's relationship with his or her therapist and how these are (socially) constructed by both parties. It can also be used to consider ways in which counsellors articulate therapeutic values or construct and 'defend' approaches to practice, supervision or ongoing personal and professional development. Discourse analysis is concerned with etymology (the history and use of words); in this sense it is used to develop arguments from particular, often 'radical' and emancipatory, standpoints that critically examine, articulate and challenge language that is used in and about therapy, in an attempt to generate knowledge, and promote equality and social justice. While recognising the strengths of such an emancipatory position in the critique and challenge of particular experiences and constructs, we must also see the challenge of objectivity – or its lack. Critical discursive arguments are often generated without due consideration of the particular ontological and axiological position of the researcher; this needs to be deliberated by both reader and researcher who wish to be assured of the integrity and validity of research processes and outputs.

The first stage in the process of discourse analysis is for researchers to read and immerse themselves in the transcribed data (data that is relevant – however, ensure that nothing of potential significance is missed). Data is then reflexively coded (noting personal, intuitive responses to the data) in light of the research question, enabling extracts of the data to be identified that can be iteratively subjected to further interrogation and analysis. Aspects of the transcripts can be read and reread in different ways with different emphases in order to enable continuing insight. Language, patterns and figures of speech, including the use of paralanguage and metaphors, are examined and contextualised in order to create critical meaning, which can be critiqued from particular social and philosophical standpoints (see Willig, 2009). Discursive analysis as an approach therefore promotes understanding of how phenomena are intersubjectively experienced, constructed and articulated within specific contexts, and considers ways in which the narrowness of particular discourses might be challenged.

ACTIVITY 5.7

Let us consider discourse analysis as applied to counselling. We might argue, for example, that counselling is predominantly a middle-class activity, which has developed from progressive, liberal, middle-class values; that most counselling students and practitioners are female and middle-aged; and that the majority of clients are also female.

- Note for yourself the challenges this raises. What are the resultant dominant discourses? What might be challenged? What might be researched further? How might discourse analysis be utilised? What might you need to consider reflexively? Share your thoughts in a group discussion.

Narrative analysis

You will doubtless be familiar with the childhood refrain: 'Are you sitting comfortably? Then we shall begin . . .'. Stories are central to life; they enable us to construct and convey meaning, through plots, characters and scenes; they help us to develop an understanding of ourselves and our place in the world. Narrative has the powerful capacity to evoke emotion, and to transport us to new, exciting, unexplored and even unimagined places through a range of genre, imagery and metaphor. Stories give us the opportunity to understand and conceptualise experience (Bruner, 1990) and to organise *everyday interpretations of the world in storied form* (Murray, 2009, p112); they allow us to go beyond passive recipience to become active co-constructers of meaning (ibid.). They create space to understand those meanings in *forms and functions [that] are situationally rooted in culture contexts, scenes and events which give meaning to action* (Cohen et al., 2011, p455). Narrative work enables the conveyance of lived realities that have the capacity to elicit rich and enriching data. Life in the postmodern world only guarantees uncertainty; for many, however, the greater social freedoms and multiple truth possibilities that are experienced enable the construction and sculpting of personal biographies through interactions and personal life choices, to which meaning is attached through shared storying. It is through these stories that *order and meaning [are brought] to everyday life* (Murray, 2009, p115) in the reflexive construction of selfhood.

In counselling, clients use narrative to convey meaning; therapists of different orientations use these narratives in different ways to make psychological contact, empathically enter their clients' worlds, challenge thought patterns, establish causality, thematise and make connections between present and past. Narrative therapy as a psychotherapeutic approach engages clients in the construction of parallel and multiple storied alternatives (Mair, 1989). Clients are invited to examine other possibilities of how their stories might be viewed through separating the clients from presenting issues in such a way as to externalise them and to de-problematise the clients themselves. In this way clients are invited to re-author their lives, and to write alternative futures to the storylines that have been written to this point.

In therapeutic work, the structure with which clients narrate their stories is of interest. Some clients chronologise the past in order to contextualise the present; for others the opposite is true, while others still boundary their story microcosmically in the present and recent past. Then there are the stories that appear to seamlessly and effortlessly zoom and connect between different time zones. Each client story also presents a unique trajectory to future experience, hopes and aspirations. Chronology then can be a helpful, but not restrictive, framework within which to explore and understand narrative. It is the function of narrative inquiry to make sense of stories, and how they are intertwined with other stories (including our own) in creating a contextual tapestry or backdrop that brings characters, plots, scenes, interconnections and contexts to life. It is this that enables the reader to engage with the story in all its colours, sounds, tastes, smells, textures, thoughts and feelings. In this sense, not only are research participants engaged in telling their own stories, they are joined by the researchers who become co-narrators in constructing joint narratives that seek to make sense of the participants' worlds and the contexts in which they are situated. It is in this way that *we can begin to understand the narrators and their worlds* (Murray, 2009, p116), thereby *representing people's stories as told by them* (Etherington, 2004, p75). It is the researcher's job to retell the participant's story as he or she has told and chronicled it to the researcher in such a way that honours the story and its teller (Finlay and Evans, 2009). Researchers, as Finlay reminds us, need to be aware of the 'hermeneutic turn' (Smith et al., 2009) – that participants' narratives are their own narratives of experience, which researchers in turn understand from their own frameworks and seek to convey to readers, who in turn have their own particular ways of interpreting them. The co-constructed window through which we view narrative research must therefore be acknowledged (Finlay and Evans, 2009).

Counselling is a site of storytelling, a place where clients retell their own stories in order to challenge, understand and rewrite them with the help of another. As such, the cathartic nature of storytelling is universally accepted within the therapeutic world (Etherington, 2009). Counsellors too, within appropriate ethical and professional boundaries, engage in retelling stories of therapy and therapeutic processes; therapy in different ways embodies storytelling. Narrative research approaches therefore align well with counselling and counselling research (ibid.) in *capturing the detailed stories of life experiences of a single life or the lives of a small number of individuals* (Cresswell, 2007, p55).

ACTIVITY 5.8

- Think about your favourite story; what qualities do you appreciate? Write these down.
- How might you foster some of these qualities within a piece of narrative analysis?

Narrative inquiry, as we have noted, is grounded in participants' stories, whether they be stories told directly, or stories told in therapy through analysis of transcripts (McLeod, 2011b). Some versions of narrative research seek to contextualise the particular research question very broadly within the participant's complete life story (what we might call a 'lifecourse' approach) in order to understand at a deeper level contextual factors and interconnections between different elements of that narrative. Other approaches seek to focus more directly on a particular event or sequence of episodes pertaining to the research question. In both cases Flick (2010, p178) reminds us of the *generative* nature of narrative inquiry; that is, researchers ask participants to generate their own stories for the purposes of the research. In lifecourse analysis, the generative question would be very open:

> *Please tell me the story of your life and how it happened. Perhaps the most effective way to do this would be to start from birth and work chronologically to the present day. I realise that this will take some time, but I would like to encourage you not to rush, as I would like to understand your story as you understand it, to understand from your perspective the things that are of importance to you.*

In episodic narrative inquiry, the generative question must be framed sufficiently broadly to give permission for the research participant to explore his or her story in order that interconnections can be suitably made to the topic under investigation, while doing so in a manner that emphasises the story's relationship to the research question itself, in order that the informant is encouraged to develop the threads of his or her narrative to that end (ibid.).

Thus:

1. 'Please tell me the story of your life and how it happened. Perhaps the most effective way to do this would be to start from birth and work chronologically to the present day. I would like you to feel free to tell me as much about yourself and your experiences in life as you feel able.'
2. 'I am interested in your experiences of therapy; what caused you to come, how you found the process, how you feel about the outcome; I wonder if you might be able to describe any significant moments for you in counselling?'

Narrative research accounts can be collected in a variety of ways. These include spending time with research informants and encouraging them to retell their stories through multiple media (observation, photographs, video, quilts, scrapbooks, letters, artwork, music, etc.). The primary research tool, however, is the interview. The researcher records these interactions audio-visually and by utilising a research journal to record 'field notes'. Narratives, as we have noted, are not located in a *vacuum* (Murray, 2009, p116), but rather are contextualised by particular personal, social and cultural backdrops (ibid.; see also Cresswell, 2007). The researcher therefore needs to offer rich and sympathetic descriptions of research participants and the contextual frameworks that narratives inhabit.

Given the timescale that many undergraduate and Master's students face, it is likely, if adopting a narrative approach, that interviews (or a series of interviews) would be the primary and most pragmatic data collection method to consider. In this case, the process of carrying out narrative research is as shown in Table 5.2 opposite.

One of the key aspects of narrative research is *restorying* (Cresswell, 2007, p56), in which the researcher retells the participant's story in a way that makes sense of the different subplots that emerge during data collection and analysis. This aspect of the research may also chronologise the story. Restorying further enables the research to be contextualised within personal, sociocultural, political and psychotherapeutic frames. The researcher begins analytical deduction of the type of story that has been told, examining it in light of its tone and genre. He or she will need to extract and examine recurring themes, metaphors and storylines, describing and offering through

Step
1. Interview participants using a schedule (as above), which encourages them to tell their stories.
2. The interview data from a number of participants are collated and common themes are generated that are representative of the cohort's stories.
3. A smaller number of participants is selected for more detailed analysis – those whose stories seem to broadly represent the data themes.
4. This smaller number of respondents' stories are transcribed and analysed in greater detail.
5. The research report is compiled by using verbatim the narratives generated alongside contextual and analytical comments that created a contextual framework for the research.

Table 5.2: Narrative research process (after Riessman, 2008; McLeod, 2011b)

critical synthesis with other data sources the issues that influence the development of the participant's story (Hennink et al., 2011).

Narrative research holds sacrosanct the collaboration between researcher and the researched; this extends to the ongoing engagement of research participants in the process of both restorying the research and checking the validity of the work. This ongoing collaboration can also act as a catalyst in generating further narrative material and in elucidating further causal links in the data (Cresswell, 2007). In presenting the analysed data, extended excerpts of transcripts (including paralanguage) are produced verbatim and punctuated by the researcher's analytical commentary, which seeks to frame the participant's story within the wider contexts of the research question, while enabling the researcher to articulate his or her own reflexive engagement. Much narrative research is written in the present (with appropriate use of other tenses for contrast), in order to elicit a 'here and now' rather than 'then and there' effect.

The following is an extract from an excellent example of narrative research by Kim Etherington (2009), in which two research participants retell their stories of the therapeutic benefits of being involved in a previous piece of research (Etherington, 2007) that explored links between traumatic experience and drug use. In this excerpt we are clearly able to view a co-narration of one of the participants' stories as told by (Omar) himself. This narrative is supported reflexively and contextually by the researcher (Kim).

Example – Omar and Kim

Second meeting

It had taken almost six weeks for us to arrange our second meeting. In the meantime I had sent Omar the transcript of our first meeting and suggested that we both read it prior to meeting again. When we met I inquired how he had been feeling about our previous conversation and he answered:

Omar: Actually since the last time we met . . . I've been talking to my therapist about my anxiety as a child. Now it fits into place with my dad's violent behaviour, and I had never made the connection before. It's really odd – I've never looked at it that way.

Kim: So you hadn't made that connection in previous therapy?

Omar: No, no . . .

Kim: It seemed to come up quite late in the conversation didn't it? I was quite surprised.

Omar: Yes, it's almost like I'd blocked it out really. It's like it's there, but isn't there – but now it's very visible to me that that was going on and it was very scary for me as a child.

I was curious about how our conversation had helped him to make those connections when therapy had not. So I asked him how he saw the differences and/or similarities between our research conversations and his therapy/ counselling.

Omar: Yes, I don't see it as counselling. It has its similarities, but no, I think it's really me restructuring or mapping, it's almost like mapping my whole life, and . . . yes, putting it together, because it is pretty much all over the place. And I don't think in therapy you get that opportunity – well I haven't really – unless you're given some sort of homework or a timeline or something . . .

Kim: So the telling of the story meant that you needed to order it. And I've helped you with that a bit in saying, 'What happened then?', or, 'How old were you when that happened?' That's kind of kept you a bit on track?

Omar: Yes definitely . . . it's almost like a jigsaw puzzle, like missing pieces making more connections. It's been a very useful experience. I keep thinking about emailing it [transcript] to my sponsor, just so he can get a real good insight into what's been going on. Like I say, I keep keying in on that part about the connection with the anxiety as a child – that has baffled me for years . . . and it sounds so simple after hearing what was going on in my life with the violence. It was just like, 'of course – that was what was going on in my life!' I feel relieved . . . it's funny really, it's brought up a lot for me, yes. It's therapy but it's not therapy.

Kim: It's therapeutic, but it's not therapy. But there's also something different in the relationship isn't there? . . . In the research relationship I think it's easier to meet as kind of collaborators, colleagues, equals: I need something from you and you're helping me out here, whereas in therapy you come as the one who needs help. I think that has an impact on the power relationships.

Omar: Yes, absolutely, that's a really good point . . . yes, the dynamics are completely different. I mean, when I'm talking to my therapist it's very different . . .

Kim: In what way?

Omar: I think I feel a bit more pressured when I'm in therapy. I feel a bit more relaxed here, in expressing my story. In the therapeutic relationship it's very much more . . . I don't know, not much to say, it's more fearful, I'm scared I'm going to be analysed about something. I'm watching for it really. . . . Yes, I do hold back with him, and I don't know – is that because he's a man or we haven't built up a complete trust? Last week he made a comment to me: he said, maybe you want to start trusting me sooner or later? So he's very aware of it as well.

REFLECTION POINT

- How do your clients utilise narrative within therapy? How is therapy co-constructed as a result of that narrative?
- What narratives about therapy might you, your clients and your supervisor 'tell' within the therapeutic system about therapy itself? How might this be helpful?
- Do any of the research ideas that you are considering 'fit' with a narrative research approach?

As we have seen, narrative approaches to counselling research provide a powerful vehicle that runs parallel to therapeutic work itself. Narrative inquiry enables the co-construction of stories that are contextualised within the participant's own lifecourse and wider socially constructed discourses that reflexively influence the ongoing direction of the biography.

GROUNDED THEORY

We might be familiar with maxims such as: 'Texting is the new talking . . . *or so the theory goes.*' Theory underpins much thinking and practice in both the scientific and social worlds. The challenge for any researcher (particularly the qualitative researcher) is to consider how theoretical ideas are formed and validated. In counselling we involve and evolve theory as frameworks to conceptualise practice, which in turn inform and enable us to reflect on what we do in the therapeutic space. Theory provides the hook on which we can hang pictures of practice, a means to articulate ideas on human nature, thought, behaviour, development, capacity and change. Counselling theories generate describable and sustained rationales for particular praxes, which can in turn become justificatory mechanisms for different therapeutic interventions. Theories then are important, but we might argue that they cannot and should not be fixed; that we should provide the space and conditions for theoretical ideas to be challenged and new perspectives on therapeutic phenomena to grow and develop. Over time theories can become engrained in the common psyche, and resultantly risk becoming urban, academic or therapeutic myth. Grounded theory enables the researcher to go beyond conceptualised fables and *generate or discover a theory* (Creswell, 2007, p63) that is generated from, and robustly validated by, participants' empirical experiences.

Grounded theory was developed by Chicago-based sociologists Barney Glaser and Anselm Strauss in the 1960s. They were concerned with theorising experiences of death and dying from a sociological perspective and wanted to build a framework that offered a theory on this subject within a given time and space that remained true to their participants' experiences. Grounded theory draws on a range of traditions, including positivism and symbolic interactionism, a sociological approach that is concerned with how people microcosmically interact to make meaning and construct reflexive identities. For many, grounded theory is a bridge between positivist and interpretivist epistemologies. It seeks to construct generalisable theories through a process of 'saturating' a theoretically selected data sample on a given phenomenon (Cresswell, 2007). Grounded theory is attractive to many student researchers as it provides a systematic, step-by-step approach to inquiry and addresses positivist challenges about the transparency and rigour of qualitative inquiry while embracing the *creative elements of emergent discovery* (Hennink et al., 2011, p207).

The notion of emergence is important here; it entails a process of inductive discovery (as opposed to deductive hypothesising), which remains true to its interactionist roots in which people are viewed as social actors who are involved in the active construction of their own personal meanings and biographies. Hennink and colleagues therefore note: *uncovering the process through which this happens is fundamental to the grounded theory approach* (ibid.). Hence grounded theory employs active and 'becoming' language. It is a methodology that is helpful and appropriate where the researcher might wish to (re)test, challenge or augment existing theory or where there is little current knowledge or literature relating directly to the research topic (Denscombe, 2010).

Grounded theorists are likely to employ a sample size of between eight and twenty participants. Traditionally in line with its positivist roots, a grounded theorist will seek to engage with the data in an objective manner that, as fully as possible, ignores a priori knowledge on the subject under investigation. The literature review in grounded theory research therefore occurs after all of the empirical data have been gathered and analysed. The challenge with this, of course, is that the researcher is likely to be familiar with at least some of the professional literature related to the topic being researched. Throughout the process, the grounded theorist is encouraged to engage in a process of *reflexive memoing*, which enables him or her to map ideas, bracket personal biases, and consider other influences on the research, including prior personal, professional and academic knowledge (Creswell, 2007). Memoing, therefore, provides an audit trail that aids transparency and validity. More recently other brands of grounded theory have emerged that helpfully recognise the involved role of the researcher within the research process, as opposed to the passive objective bystander approach espoused by earlier grounded theorists. Most notable among these newer grounded theory models is a *social constructionist* approach, which has been championed, among others, by Charmaz (2006). Charmaz has sought to highlight the centrality of localised, personal, social, economic and praxes contexts through which people interact to construct individual and collective meaning to *reach a negotiated understanding of reality* (Luca, 2009, p199). Charmaz's view is therefore that theory is not so much discovered, rather that grounded theory can enable the contextualised construction of *theories that are grounded in the field and in the data* (Flick, 2010, p429).

In commencing a grounded theory study, the researcher will seek to frame a research question that is *broad, open-ended and action-orientated* (McLeod, 2011b, p120). The researcher will analyse and code every transcript, noting emergent theoretical ideas; in light of this and where deemed appropriate, the researcher may alter the interview schedule before re-entering the field in order to 'test' what is evolving, thus enabling the generation of further codes. This is an iterative process that is akin to developing theory through *snowballing* – of gathering more and more evidence that supports and refines emergent ideas. Flick describes this process as *a spiral of cycles of data collection, coding, analysis, writing, design, theoretical categorisation and data collection* (2010, p428). The researcher will use individual transcripts in order to examine meaning units and attach open codes that seek to represent each participant's experience of the subject being discussed. Grounded theory seeks to explore alternative action-orientated meanings in line with its interactionist epistemology, before themes within each data item (transcript) are clustered and interconnections (of cause and effect) between themes are made through *axial coding*. Grounded theory analysis involves a process of deconstructing each transcript in order to understand its finer detail, and reconstructing it to examine causality with the additional clarity generated through the process of open coding (McLeod, 2011b). Each transcript is analysed in this way as the researcher returns to and from the research field to examine each interview in turn to make and note connections within and across data items. The process concludes when no further iteration is possible and data saturation is reached (i.e. no new insights or themes are generated by the analysis). At this point the researcher needs to generate a central causal category that captures and conceptualises the dynamic interrelationships between actors and phenomena in the data. The theory the researcher generates must be representative of, supported by and grounded in the empirical data (see Figure 5.3).

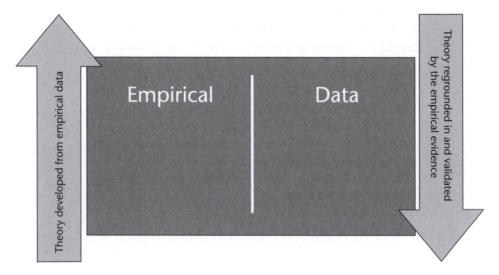

Figure 5.3: Empirical data

Grounded theory as an approach is one that many students do find helpful. It is well defined, with a clear and rationalised step-by-step approach to its execution. It has the potential to produce new perspectives and theories that are firmly based in the empirical evidence generated through a purposive sampling approach. It rebuffs much of the criticism espoused by positivists; however, we should note that, in its attempts to generate empirically supported theory that, in its approach, straddles positivist and interpretivist positions, grounded theory can potentially risk generating a generalised, theorised and reductionist worldview that may lose or not do full justice to the nuances of each participant's lived experience – a challenge to which would-be grounded theorists should rise.

ETHNOGRAPHIC APPROACHES

Ethnography

Ethnography as a research methodology is grounded in anthropology and especially the work of some late nineteenth-century anthropologists who studied pre-industrial societies (Silverman, 2009). The term 'ethnography' is derived from 'ethno', meaning peoples, and 'graph', meaning writing, and therefore is concerned with providing written records about different people groups. Given the picture that is perhaps engendered of Western researchers arriving in 'uncivilised' societies wearing jungle hats and shorts in order to study and write about native communities, we might perceive ethnography as somehow being concerned with capturing the experience of 'otherness'. With this in mind, it is important that researchers are aware and effectively convey something of themselves and their position within ethnographic work in order that the essential nature of the group or culture under investigation is authentically expressed. In this vein, ethnographers, as with other qualitative approaches, are encouraged to keep personal research diaries that map their own personal experiences of their engagement in the research field in order to enhance the reflexivity and validity of their work. Ethnographers are required to immerse themselves over time in their research field (albeit in different ways according to rationalised positions that we will outline), in order to construct a reality of how individuals and groups interact within different social settings, and to convey how participants understand their worlds (Denscombe, 2008).

Ethnography assumes a social constructionist position, which avows that social realities and identities are continually constructed through actors' actions and interactions within particular institutions and settings. As such, ethnography pays a deal of attention to the significance of the particular ideographic context in which the research is situated; data is *socially situated, context-related, context-dependent and context-rich* (Cohen et al., 2011, p219). Flick argues that *the theoretical background here is the analysis of the production of social reality from an external perspective* (2010, p225). While it is true that ethnography has its roots in studying what might be considered the 'novel' or even 'exotic' lifestyles of different cultures, it has more recently been accepted and valued as a methodological approach in capturing naturalistic evidence that embraces 'everydayness'. Much ethnography places the researcher at the centre of the research process over an extended period and allows him or her to use a range of data collection methods, including observation and interviews; it is an embodied approach that enables the researcher to use all of his or her physical senses to experience and express the social reality of participants' worlds.

The position of the researcher is integral to the particular ethnographic approach adopted. For some, ethnography is concerned with the generation of highly naturalistic data that is primarily generated through observation (Sanders and Wilkins, 2010). In this instance, researchers need to position themselves as objective bystanders who minimally (if at all) engage with the study cohort so as not to influence or infect the naturally occurring social processes that they seek to observe. This we might think of as non-participant observation. This form of ethnography crosses positivist and interpretivist epistemological positions. The researcher will work with predetermined codes and record instances of behaviour or interactions that fit into the coding system. Additionally, the researcher *may* record qualitative aspects that do not specifically fit the coding system that has been generated. This covert ethnographic approach seeks to generate objective data that is free from the bias of researcher intervention or presence; however, it does raise ethical issues about the lack of participant informed consent, something that is additionally noteworthy in counselling research, given its particular professional concerns with the ethics of trust and confidentiality. That said, some research using this particular approach has been undertaken in counselling through analysis of live therapy sessions where researchers have conducted their analysis in adjoining rooms.

A second ethnographic position is that of the observer-participant. In this instance, the researcher is introduced to the research participants in his or her research capacity, but retains separateness from the study cohort. *It is a type of conscious journalistic approach to observation in which the researcher reports on the action from the privileged position of researcher without having to get involved* (ibid., p165). While, of course, this approach is ethically more transparent, it does leave open to debate the impact of the very presence of someone known to be a researcher on research participants' behaviours and the naturalness of the interactions that the researcher seeks to capture and understand within his or her given social context.

A third position is where the researcher makes clear his or her role as a researcher at the commencement of the research process, before, through a process of observation and action, becoming assimilated into norms and practices of the research cohort in order to study and report it experientially from 'the inside'. This effectively strikes the balance between certain ethical and research concerns, and may be an appropriate approach for those wishing to conduct an ethnographic study on their own or on another counselling agency. It must be noted, though, that the duality of roles within this approach needs to be considered. Sanders and Wilkins note: *it puts strain on the observer being in two roles* (ibid., p166). Furthermore, if conducting ethnographic research with counsellors who you may know, there remains the risk that the naturalness of the research might be compromised if people know they are being observed for a particular purpose *thereby disturbing or influencing the action as it develops* (ibid.). McLeod reminds us of the *challenge to maintain an appropriate balance between involvement and distance* (1999, p102), thereby arguing the difficulty, but not the impossibility of conducting an ethnographic study within one's own counselling agency or setting. Here, however, further ethical concerns arise when reporting (however well anonymised) the actions or behaviours of others or the culture of an organisation to which the researcher might well belong.

The final approach that the ethnographer might adopt is that of full participant. In this approach the researcher endeavours to surreptitiously become a full member of the group by concealing his identity in order to study it covertly. Being part of the group in this way enables the researcher to participate in its lived reality and to observe how meaning is constructed and enacted from the inside. As those being observed are unaware of the researcher's true identity and purpose, they are more likely to behave naturally; however, the influence of the researcher as a *person* cannot be accounted for. This, however, presents ethical concerns which include, yet go beyond the usual issues of informed consent. To what extent, for example, is it appropriate for the researcher to engage in unethical or even illegal behaviours in order to further his research purposes? What are the ethical implications of potential over-engagement which might be generated through such full participation? What might be the impact on the researcher's sense of self, and indeed, of the researcher's 'footprint' on the study cohort?

Clearly in observing others we end up observing ourselves. Ethnographers need to develop significant levels of reflexivity in order to aid objectivity in their work, and to be aware of how they use themselves in interpreting observations.

Denscombe reminds and challenges us that:

> As researchers, the meanings we attach to things that happen and the language we use to describe them are the product of **our own** culture, social background and personal experiences. Making sense of what is observed during fieldwork observation is a process that relies on what the researcher already knows and already believes, and it is not a voyage of discovery which starts from a clean sheet . . . The question that taxes ethnographers is this: 'How can my description of the culture or event depict things from the point of view of those involved when I can only use my own way of seeing things, my own conceptual tools, to make sense of what is happening?'
>
> (2008, p68; emphasis added)

Flick (2010) notes that the process of generating ethnographic data should begin with rich contextual description, before moving towards:

> Focused observation [that] narrows your perspective on those processes and problems, which are most essential for your research question [before commencing] selective evaluation [that] is focused on finding further evidence and examples for the types of practices and processes which are being observed and articulated in the research.
>
> Spradley (1980, p34, as cited in Flick, 2010, p227)

There are aspects of ethnography that, of course, run parallel to therapy; the counsellor is engaged in making sense of his or her client's (or client group's) world through observing, sensing and interviewing over an extended period of weeks or months, and reporting something of that ethnographic experience through therapy notes and supervision. Dallos and Vetere remind us that: . . . *in the process of therapy we have to engage in a very complex process wherein we observe our clients – how they look, their posture, facial expressions, tone of voice, movement and so on* (2005, p161).

ACTIVITY 5.9

Consider ways in which you might use or integrate an ethnographic approach into your research.

- Is this appropriate? What challenges might you face?
- How might you address the concerns raised in Martyn Denscombe's quotation above?

Ethnographic approaches to counselling and psychotherapy research remain valid and possible for many counselling students. However, given the additional complexity of the particular ethical issues that ethnographic approaches might engender in counselling research, researchers need to develop a clear and well-defined rationale for their use and execution. Overt ethnography, more than most qualitative approaches, raises questions about access to participants. It is largely impossible to commence ethnographic fieldwork without the assistance of others who can help researchers gain access to appropriate settings and people who might be willing to engage in such research processes. The influence of these gatekeepers is likely to continue throughout the research process, and researchers can find themselves trying to maintain the goodwill of these people in order to ensure ongoing access to the field, while assuring that their influence does not unduly bias the research. Dallos and Vetere (2005, p169) argue the importance of *reciprocity* in the field, and that the cooperation of gatekeeper or organisation should be recognised, perhaps by agreeing to present the report findings. This also needs to be handled with care, particularly if the findings may detail some critical or unwelcome conclusions. Notwithstanding these points, ethnographic research has the powerful potential to provide rich and insightful perspectives, generated from inside the study cohort, which can elucidate client experience and counselling practices and cultures.

Autoethnography

As we have noted, the application of ethnographic processes requires researchers to immerse themselves fully in the data collection and analysis. It is in a very real sense a form of incarnational research, a way of living with participants and the data that is embodied within particular social or organisational contexts, enabling researchers to understand the particular socially constructed mechanisms with which participants view and enact their worlds. In this way, researchers are situated within the research and must reflexively engage with fluxing locations in order to make sense of their research for their participants, their readers and themselves. Whereas ethnography is the explicit observation of others with implicit, but nonetheless expressed, observation of the researcher's self, autoethnography is concerned with the deliberate and explicit, reflexive *and* objective study of oneself within particular contexts. Autoethnography is therefore *a form of self-narrative that places the self within a social context* (Etherington, 2004, pp140–1), in an attempt to understand the recursive interplay between the self and sociocultural contexts. In autoethnography the researcher becomes the researched.

Much about therapy, as we have noted in Chapter 2, engages us in the 'use of self' (Rowan and Jacobs, 2011; Wosket, 2011); autoethnography encourages us to bring that self *to* and write about that self *as* a subject of research. In this way autoethnography can be viewed as a memoir of concentrated personal processes that enables deep and transformative reflective learning to occur (Bager-Charleson, 2010; Bolton, 2010). It becomes a place to map and make sense of the terrain of personal and professional experience (Wright and Bolton, 2012) and a space to invite others to share in reflections of that journey. Stories are therapeutic. Placing therapists at the centre of their own research is a cathartic endeavour not only for the therapist-researchers themselves, but potentially for their readers and the wider therapeutic community through the conveyance of *newly discovered self-knowledge* (Etherington, 2004, p145) with which others might identify. It provides a space to express personal thoughts on particular processes and phenomena in an ordered (sometimes chaotic) yet creative way, thereby enabling the writer to get in touch with and feed the self that he or she uses in therapy. The reflective processes with which autoethnographers engage bring self into consciousness (Zahavi, 2008). Practically speaking, autoethnography in this sense becomes a focused extension of the type of journaling that many therapists engage in as part of their own personal and professional development – and which is a requirement of many counselling training programmes. Autoethnography doesn't only involve the storying of self through the written word; autoethnographers frequently use different media, including video, photographs, pictures, paintings, music, poetry, lyrics, fabrics, etc., all of which have the power to convey something of the personal narrative of the writer. Autoethnography is heuristic (Moustakas, 1990); it enables the researcher to explore an aspect of profound personal experience or meaning at depth, in order to birth new insight that is then shared with and corroborated by others. The narrative approach employed is designed to *allow the reader or audience to enter the experience itself . . . to create the possibility for the audience to construct its own interpretation and understanding of the material* (McLeod, 2011b, pp209–10). Autoethnographers therefore need to develop a methodological approach that critiques and articulates the idea of self and considers the particular constructs of the self that they are able to own for themselves. It is these 'selves' that provide a frame for the potentially rich and colourful tapestries that are often woven in auto-ethnographic studies. As Muncey states:

> *Our particular sense of self comes from a combination of our biological flow, our social context, our bodily awareness and our specific consciousness. We are aware that an important part of the self is a private inner world of thoughts, feelings and fantasies which we only share if we choose to. We recognise a continuity from our younger selves but there is also a sense that we are continually renewed.*
>
> (2011, p11)

Autoethnography has faced the charge of being *self-indulgent* (Etherington, 2004, p141), and runs the risk of being so unless researchers are able to articulate something of its wider academic value and its axiological position as an appropriate postmodern, subversive, biographical methodology, which *seeks to question and challenge structures of knowledge that are used to maintain relationships of power and control in society* (McLeod, 2011b, p210). An example of this is cited in Muncey (2011), who sought to contest the socially constructed normative worldview of teenage mothers as morally and socially deficient. Autoethnography therefore draws on and has the capacity to sit between a wide range of ontological positions and epistemological approaches, including narrative, phenomenology, heuristic, postmodern and gendered theories, enabling the writer to generate work that is both a personal critique and unique representation of the author's own lifeworld experience of a given phenomenon within particular socially constructed worldviews.

So much of qualitative research is in some way connected to the researcher as a 'self'. As we have seen earlier in Erica's case study (see page 64), questions that arise frequently come from a place associated with the researcher's personal or professional life. Autoethnography on its own, or bricolaged with other methodologies, gives the researcher the opportunity and challenge to appropriate and make explicit those selves within research in a way that often elicits a process of rich personal discovery and deep professional learning that enlivens qualitative research work.

ACTIVITY 5.10

In Activity 5.3, you were asked to interview a colleague about why he or she decided to become a therapist. Reflect on this autoethnographically for yourself. You might, for example, note over the next few weeks what continues to motivate you in your practice today.

- What are the sounds, tastes, sights and sensations that arise in your conscious awareness?
- How might these match or challenge your own particular socially constructed view of the world as formed through your other narrative selves?

This, of course, is one example. You are likely to be forming other research ideas and questions, and if this is the case, you might consider applying the questions above to that research kernel.

INTERPRETATIVE PHENOMENOLOGICAL ANALYSIS

Interpretative Phenomenological Analysis (IPA) was initially developed by Professor Jonathan Smith, a psychologist at Birkbeck University of London in the 1990s. It is a qualitative approach that has gathered significant kudos in the social sciences and in counselling research in recent years. IPA draws on both phenomenology (the study of human experience) and hermeneutics (the study of interpretation), thus placing the researcher dynamically in the roles of empathic co-experiencer *and* research-interrogator. IPA studies therefore seek to produce research that is richly grounded in participants' experiences, yet maintains a critical interpretivist position that further interrogates meaning within particular social constructions that are relevant to the research.

The foundation of IPA

The founding father of phenomenology was the German psychologist and philosopher Edmund Husserl (1859–1938). Husserl's work at the beginning of the twentieth century challenged some of the prevailing ideas in psychological research, which reduced human experience to different forms of learned behaviour. Smith et al. note that *The founding principle of phenomenological inquiry is that experience should be examined in the way that it occurs, and in its own terms* (2009, p12). Phenomenologists therefore value the multiple realities that people construct and are concerned with viewing others' worlds as they themselves do. Phenomenology *provide[s] a description of how things are experienced first hand by those involved*

(Denscombe, 2008, p76). It is concerned with consciousness, the ways in which experiences are understood and how meanings are constructed as a result of phenomena.

It is this idea of lived experience in the everyday world, or what Husserl referred to as *lifeworld*, that concerns phenomenologists to whom reality is individually subjective. In this way phenomenological research approaches seek to offer a transcendental vehicle through which individual and collective meanings are richly expressed and understood. While recognising subjective reality, phenomenologists hold that a real world exists beyond individual consciousness and that we are engaged in an intentional relationship (what Husserl called 'intentionality') with that world through which we interpret both it and ourselves (Spinelli, 2010). The *phenomenological attitude* (Smith et al., 2009, p12) requires the researched to turn their attention from the particular 'object' or phenomenon under discussion – to internalise and 'feel' how they experience a particular phenomenon and the meanings that they attach to it. In understanding the self therefore we understand experience, and in understanding experience we understand the self (Zahavi, 2008). Humans therefore make sense out of experience and experience out of sense. Although, as Zahavi goes on to argue, the major voices who have dominated phenomenological thinking have posited that self-consciousness streams irrespective of whether we attend to it or not, it is however in attending to it that we are more able to raise our awareness of it. It is the researcher's role, therefore, to empathically enter the research participant's world, to seek to raise consciousness and to understand the other's lifeworld as they understand it themselves. In this way research becomes a conscious collaboration between researcher and participant, which intentionally brings about description of the phenomenon being studied together with its processes and meanings. Phenomenology is therefore concerned with the essence of experience, and with seeking to convey the essential nature of meaning to others.

Hopefully you will be able to connect some of the ideas that have been developed with therapy, notably the person-centred work of Carl Rogers. Rogers premised much of his work on the phenomenological idea that each individual constructs and understands his or her own reality in a unique way. Empathy, as a Rogerian core condition, is concerned with entering the client's world and moving freely, yet carefully, around within it, seeking to understand its subjective reality and the feelings and meanings the person attaches to experience. In this way, phenomenological approaches to research are deeply appealing to counselling students – particularly those who are grounded in humanistic practice. As such, phenomenology sits well with many counselling students' humanistic axiology, which values and respects each person as an individual. Yet, as within therapy, even the deepest empathic experience is limited by intersubjectivity. No matter the depth of relationship I might have with a client, my own capacity to fully understand them as they understand themselves is restricted by the fact that I am a separate human being, and as with therapy each of us brings to research our own subjective reality of the world that is developed through a myriad of experiences and influences. In an attempt to address this, phenomenological approaches encourage the researcher to consciously and continually *bracket off* (Smith et al., 2009, p99) or *epoche* (Langdridge, 2007, p17) such personal values and beliefs about the research question and participants, in order to best understand the essential meaning as experienced by the other. In bracketing off, the researcher, like the counsellor, is able to get closer to each individual's subjective reality in a way that more fully respects the person, his or her story and the meanings the person attaches to it.

Husserl's work on phenomenology was further developed by another German philosopher, Martin Heidegger (1889–1976). Heidegger recognised the limitations of Husserl's purist phenomenology, that as human beings we live in an interpretative and interpreted world. Research participants interpret their own worlds and, despite researchers' best attempts to bracket off their own presuppositions about participants' worlds, it is not *fully* possible to do so. Thus, in effect, researchers experience what Smith et al. describe as a *double hermeneutic* (2009, p35), *because the researcher is trying to make sense of the participant trying to make sense of what is happening to them* (ibid., p3). Indeed, we might even view research as a triple hermeneutic turn: *the reader making sense of the writer making sense of the participant, making sense of X* (ibid., p41). Heidegger, therefore, began to rationalise a hermeneutic slant to phenomenology, as a means of not only making sense of the participant's world, but of also seeking to explain it to others. If we accept the assertion that we live interpreted lives in an interpreted world, we might argue that phenomenology in its purist form does not in fact exist. Phenomenology may, like objectivity, be a direction that we wish to travel or a goal to work towards, but not be truly obtainable. Heidegger recognised that researchers will, despite epoche, bring their own interpretation to different parts of the process. It is therefore essential that researchers make clear their own ontological and axiological positions on the research subject, in order that they can reflexively engage with the research process to ensure the transparency and validity of their work.

Whereas phenomenology is concerned with the purity of described meaning, hermeneutics has as its core the capacity to bring out the richness of the data through interpretation. However:

> *No matter how different phenomenology and hermeneutics may be, they possess significant areas of convergence . . . [they] both assume an active, intentional, construction of a social world and its meanings by reflexive human beings.*
>
> (McLeod, 2007b, p57)

McLeod goes on to argue that Heidegger synergised hermeneutics and phenomenology and *create[d] something that goes beyond either . . . Either approach taken on its own leaves the job 'half done'* (ibid., p62).

ACTIVITY 5.11

Read the following extract from Bright (2011, pp21–2), a piece of research that utilised IPA to examine young client-participants' experiences of the relationship between risk, school counselling and the development of resilience.

It is my belief that children and young people can experience oppression and marginalisation, and that adults are responsible for regulating childhood. This oppression is exacerbated in areas of socio-economic disadvantage which results in the experience of social exclusion and risky transitions to adulthood. I hold the position that children and young people experience relative vulnerability by virtue of their age, and that, ethically, societies have a responsibility to respond to meet the needs of [their] young in order to mitigate the effects of that vulnerability.

Think about and discuss the following questions:

• What potential biases do you note?
• How might these impact on different aspects of the research process?
• How might objectivity be promoted and maintained?

COMMENT

In approaching this research I was influenced by a range of ontological and axiological ideas that became 'interpretative lenses' through which I viewed the world. Having worked as a youth worker and a school counsellor with children and young people impacted by different forms of social disadvantage, I became interested in the sociology of risk (Beck, 1992) and in particular how this impacted on young people (Furlong and Cartmel, 2007). In order to develop the validity of the work, I had to acknowledge and bracket my own worldviews. For me, naming my own 'biases' formed through a range of different constructed experiences enabled me to be more aware of (rather than deny) the ways in which my ideas might have influenced different aspects of the research, and how they might become a barrier to a closer phenomenological knowing of my participants' lifeworlds.

IPA in process

IPA maintains a strong connection to its ideographic roots, which *aim for an in-depth focus on the particular and a commitment to detailed finely textured analysis of actual life and lived experience* (Shinebourne, 2011, p47). As such, those considering an IPA approach to research need to commit *to understand[ing] experiential phenomena from the perspective of particular individuals in particular contexts* (Finlay, 2011, p140). Those adopting IPA are therefore reminded that they should resist the temptation to make grand claims about research. Typically, given that IPA seeks to engage at depth rather than breadth, most researchers will involve between three and six research participants through purposive sampling. As it is important that participants have some experience of the phenomenon in question, *IPA researchers usually try to find a fairly homogeneous sample, for whom the research question will be meaningful* (Smith et al., 2009, p49). Furthermore, as we shall demonstrate in Chapter 8, IPA's phenomenological and hermeneutic foundations require the researcher to engage in detailed micro-analysis in order to extract as much phenomenological essence from interview transcripts as possible, while doing so in a manner that interrogates and challenges meanings within contextual constructs. This done properly is a time-consuming endeavour; therefore, as much as it is tempting to consider involving a larger number of participants, it is inadvisable to do so.

IPA as a phenomenological methodology is concerned with the nuances of how phenomena are experienced and made sense of. To this end, the data collection method needs to both enable the framing of the research question and allow participants space to explore different aspects of experience. It is for this reason that IPA studies tend to use semi-structured interviews, which allow *the researcher and participant to engage in a dialogue whereby initial questions are modified in the light of the participants' responses and the investigator is able to probe interesting and important areas which arise* (Smith and Osborn, 2009, p57). The interview schedule should therefore contain open questions that enable participants to explore different aspects of their own experience of the given phenomenon, with as little interruption from the interviewer as possible. That said, it can also be helpful to include prompts that help clarify the question's intent. These should only be used if the research participant is unclear about the question, as over-prompting can lead to semi-structured interviews becoming too structured, thereby restricting the participants and their range of expressed experience. For example, 'What brought you to therapy?' (Prompt: Was it a particular event?); 'How did you feel about being referred for counselling?' (Prompt: Relief, trepidation, hope?).

Like counselling, research interviews involve relationships, albeit of a different sort. Rapport and trust need to be built. It is therefore advisable to commence with open, more general questions that relate to the person and the research and move towards questions that might be more personal and specific. It is important to be familiar with the interview schedule in order that questions become a reference point rather than something that is slavishly adhered to. In this way the researcher is able to concentrate more fully on interaction with the participant, and develop more of a 'felt sense' of his or her experience in the interview. The recording of the interview also enables the researcher to engage more fully with the participant, meaning that he or she is more attuned to what *is* said and meant, rather than what might be missed. All of this helps the researcher get in touch with more vivid, richer data during the research analysis. IPA advises, indeed requires, that interviews are transcribed. Given that semi-structured interviews often take around an hour to conduct and each hour typically eight hours to transcribe, it is clear that this a time-consuming, although necessary, part of the process. In order not to 'contaminate' the analysis of subsequent transcripts, it is best to analyse each interview in turn, before transcription and analysis of the next. The researcher will need to read and reread each transcript in order to immerse him- or herself in the data. A sample template is provided in Chapter 8, and here, as you will note, we suggest completing the analysis using four columns. The transcription is placed in the first column; the researcher should slowly and systematically work through the transcript using the second column to note exploratory comments or meaning units, constantly asking 'What else is there here?' At the same time, the third column can be used to note reflexive ideas, feelings, intuitive responses and theoretical knowledge, which might enhance or indeed hinder the analysis. This is similar to the process of memoing used by grounded theorists (see page 79). After this has been completed, the researcher can begin to note emerging themes in the fourth column. Each transcript is analysed in turn, before common emergent themes are noted, clustered and subsumed into superordinate themes, which tell a 'big picture story' that represents the cohort's phenomenological experience, yet remains earthed in *each* participant's *individual* narrative.

Many counselling students find IPA's ontological position as a humanistic methodology, which allows phenomenological knowing and hermeneutic interpretation of others' experience, appealing because of its alignment to aspects of various therapeutic traditions. It provides a clear and accessible framework that enables researchers to *be creative and flexible* (Finlay, 2011, p141) in their approach to research. IPA, of course, does not make grand claims, which form generalisable knowledge; rather, it respects the phenomenological experience of individuals within ideographic contexts. IPA's hermeneutic approach to phenomenology recognises rather than limits the place of the researcher in the research; therefore, to some degree the researcher reflexively becomes part of the research. Indeed, some of the most effective counselling dissertations that I have seen have successfully managed to autoethnographically bricolage the reflexive phenomenological self-knowledge of the researcher with hermeneutic phenomenological understanding of others through IPA.

ACTIVITY 5.12

At the beginning of this chapter we referred to de Bono's *Six Thinking Hats*. We have mentioned 'White Hat thinking' in connection with positivism and 'Red Hat thinking' with regard to anti-positivism.

- This chapter has covered significant, albeit introductory, methodological ground. By trying on the 'Black Hat' of evaluation, what methodology or methodologies best suit your own ontology, axiology and particular research project?
- De Bono's 'Blue Hat' helps us to order the rest of the hats – to help us think about thinking. By putting on the 'Blue Hat', consider what steps you need to take next.

CHAPTER SUMMARY

In this chapter we have considered various epistemological ideas that ask us to think about how knowledge is constructed. These, as we have noted, are principally concerned with positivism and the nuanced differences within the family of interpretivist methodologies. We have introduced concepts that ask us to reflect on the way(s) in which we as people and counselling practitioners view the world, and reflected on some of the influences that have historically and personally predisposed the construction of particular positions.

We have also deliberated aspects of the nature of social constructionism and given thought to how personal constructs and experiences might impact on the validity of research. This has led us to think about the place of personal axiology in research, and challenged readers to consider how they might articulate these in research in order to enhance the reflexivity and validity of their work. At regular points in this chapter, readers have been asked to consider ways in which the various methodologies presented might be utilised or bricolaged within their own research, and it is hoped that these points of regular reflection may have enabled you to clarify some of your thinking on how different methodologies might be both 'owned' and used within the research that you will conduct. This, together with the presentation of de Bono's *Six Thinking Hats*, provides a useful framework that can be utilised at various points to enable researchers to order and appropriate the different types of thinking required at different points of the research process.

SUGGESTED FURTHER READING

Sanders, P and Wilkins, P (2010) *First Steps in Practitioner Research.* Ross-on-Wye: PCCS Books.

An excellent text that introduces novice researchers in counselling and healthcare professions to key research ideas.

Smith, J (ed.) (2009) *Qualitative Psychology: A practical guide to research methods.* London: Sage.

A seminal text that covers wide-ranging ground in an engaging, but accessible manner.

CHAPTER 6

Getting to grips with research

Graham Bright

CORE KNOWLEDGE

By the end of this chapter, you will be able to:

- appraise the importance of planning in research;
- analyse the role of procedural ethics and ethics committees in research practice.

A subtitle to this chapter might have been 'It seemed like a good idea at the time', a feeling that has pervaded the writing of this book for us at points! Planning is important to most endeavours, and especially to projects that are likely to take considerable time and effort. McLeod reflects that: *The research literature tends to offer a neat and tidy representation of what research is like* (2013b, p72). Research, like life, is not however always 'neat', especially for the many counselling students who juggle combinations of family, work, volunteering and the completion of other modules of study – not to mention 'life'. Creativity can be found in the chaos; often, however, students experience a struggle with the enormity of the research task because of a lack of planning.

There is no doubt that undertaking a piece of research is a considerable task even for the most seasoned of researchers. All research, therefore, requires good organisation in order to 'oil the wheels' and to do justice to the process. The capacity to undertake research is not only a graduate attribute, it is a professional one. As such, practitioner-researchers need to approach research with the same levels of diligence, forethought and reflexive creativity with which they engage in therapeutic practice. As in therapy, the practitioner-researcher becomes absorbed in moment-by-moment processes. Both therapy and research are sites of multiple and simultaneous interactions, which need to be 'captured' in order that deeper learning can be fostered. Mills (2010) argues that engaging in research is a form of intellectual craftsmanship, an analogy that suggests the development of creativity, skill and organisation. Such artistry requires researchers to *organise their experience*

. . . *[and to keep their] inner world awake* (ibid., p140). These ideas resonate with a certain type of order or mindful discipline, which is harnessed alongside the creative craft of research in producing high-quality work. Practically, as we have suggested in Chapter 1, this can be helped by keeping a research diary or a well-ordered research file (physically and/or electronically) in which materials pertaining to different aspects of the study can be retained and easily retrieved.

In many instances, students are required to complete a research proposal, which is often an assessed piece attached to a preparatory research methodologies module. This type of exercise is viewed not only as a summative assessment in its own right, but also as a helpful formative task that prepares students for dissertations. Proposals require students to consider the appropriate formulation of research questions, address ethical concerns, demonstrate a sound understanding of research methodologies and their applications and offer a brief review of the extant literature. Research proposals therefore act as *statement[s] of intent* (Layder, 2013, p67) and as formative frameworks to the business of research engagement. In this way, students are able to receive feedback on the constructive alignment of their work – that is, that the topic of research inquiry has generated suitable, researchable questions, that the methodology and data collection methods are fit for their intended purpose, and that intended research processes are suitably underpinned by ethical principles.

It is often the magnitude of the research task, however, that leads to creeping inertia. For many, the perceived size of the task can seem overwhelming. While not wishing to devalue or underestimate what is involved, the task of producing a 10,000–20,000-word dissertation at undergraduate or Master's level is made more manageable by considering research in its constituent parts and planning the development of the research accordingly.

ACTIVITY 6.1

- Brainstorm with a partner the different components and processes involved in research.

It is likely that the list you generated will include some of the following:

- thinking about a topic of interest;
- generating suitable research questions;
- selecting and justifying the research design and methodological approach(es);
- choosing appropriate data collection methods;
- selecting a sample;

- negotiating access to the sample;
- reviewing the literature;
- obtaining 'ethical clearance';
- choosing whether to undertake a pilot study;
- gathering data;
- analysing data;
- generating discussion that critically synthesises primary and secondary materials;
- drafting and redrafting the report;
- submitting the research;
- disseminating the findings.

The above list may still seem daunting but is hopefully more manageable if we are able to allocate a 'rough' outline of when tasks might be completed. Most students complete their dissertations at undergraduate and Master's levels in a single semester, normally after the submission of a research proposal and ethical protocol documentation. Therefore, while much of the above list is completed during just a few short months, it is not done from a standing start as students will previously have been required to develop research questions, read methodological and subject literature and consider ethical processes. One way in which time on research projects can be managed is through 'Gantt' charts. Such charts, when produced electronically (see the example in Table 6.1), provide a basis for flexible planning in research, and enable timeframes to be recalibrated when aspects of research 'slide', as they almost inevitably do. Developing traffic light coding to denote whether an aspect of the research is not yet started (red), is underway (amber) or is complete (green) can also be of help.

ACTIVITY 6.2

- Develop a Gantt chart in order to help you manage your own research. Evaluate and develop this with others.
- How realistic is your plan? How will you use the chart?
- Have your feelings about the research changed as a result of developing a research plan in this way?

There are likely to be times in the research process when your resources become stretched. This is something that many practitioner-researchers face. It is important to know when to take a break (without rest, housework or fixing something becoming an excuse for procrastination). Listening to yourself and to others around you who you trust is important. Drawing mutual strength from peers who share something of a common journey is vital. Collaboration within conducive, open and trusting environments has

	Feb 9	16	23	March 2	9	16	23	30	April 6	13	20	27	May 5	12	19	26
Background reading	Background reading															
Generate and finalise questions		Questions														
Data collection	Negotiate access	Interviews														
Data analysis			Analyse data													
Write up: Introduction	Write up				Amend											
Write up: Literature review		Write up														
Write up: Methodology	Write up															
Write up: Results						Write up										

	Feb 9	16	23	March 2	9	16	23	30	April 6	13	20	27	May 5	12	19	26
Write up: Discussion									Write up							
Write up: Recommen-dations/conclusions											Write up					
Proof read													Proof read			
Critical feedback and peer review amendments														Feedback and amendments		
Binding														Binding		
Hand in																Hand in

Table 6.1: An example of a Gantt chart

the power to foster deeper learning and develop the seeds of inquiry into something rich and productive. Often one student will read something that may not be relevant to his or her own research, but is helpful in another's.

Group exercises and appropriately applied therapeutic skills in these contexts have the potential to help individuals gain clearer insight of processes and meanings; they can illuminate and lead to profoundly rich learning. Mutual and collaborative support has the power to generate an energy and creativity that is greater than the sum of its parts. Wenger argues that such practice . . . *does not exist in the abstract. It exists because people are engaged in actions whose meanings they negotiate with one another* (2008, p73). These groups have the potential to become collaborative research hothouses; they mirror, enrich and sustain the dynamism generated in the research field. Such collaboration, however, must be ethically boundaried, and some groups sensibly engage in generating working contracts for this specific purpose. Most higher education institutions offer students access to virtual learning environments (VLEs), which provide interactive sites (including discussion forums) away from structured lectures and seminars, and which many students experience as a 'lifeline'.

Research requires creativity and tenacity – and is an endeavour best undertaken with others. Research requires discipline; readers will each know their own commitments, and how and when they function best. Some students also find a weekly research timetable of use, in addition to the suggested Gantt chart. There can be times when researchers become absorbed in, even obsessed by, their research and others when they hate it with a passion. It can, however, be all too easy to digress; reading around the topic can lead to looking at other material that is not related to the research question in hand; it is therefore vital to retain focus and keep the research question in mind at all times. The word limit set at the start of a dissertation module can seem overwhelming; many students ask: 'How will I fill the space?' Yet it soon becomes apparent that it is not 'filling the space' that is the challenge, rather a sense of being *constrained* by the word limit. Given the limitations of time and space, therefore, student-researchers need to be realistic about what their research can achieve. From the outset, research should have a well-defined and clear focus, which is regularly revisited as a safeguard against unhelpful deviations. Research questions therefore need to be specific and clear, rather than broad and generic (White, 2009; McLeod et al., 2010). Holding these ideas proactively in mind helps researchers to maintain focus and enables a realistic appraisal of the amount of data that should be gathered and analysed, thereby aiding the manageability of the task.

It is best to approach research alive to its realities and potential pitfalls in order that good planning and active awareness can help mitigate some of the common challenges that researchers face. Finding people who have experience of the phenomenon under investigation can sometimes be difficult. Practitioner-researchers need to balance the fact that a highly specific research phenomenon might be of genuine interest and value to the profession, with the reality that such specificity might restrict the available sample. Researchers pursuing investigation of a specific research phenomenon often have to rely on 'snowballing' or word of mouth from participants about others who might be interested in taking part in a study. Professional periodicals and journals often offer space for research students to advertise for participants, while others locate contributors within local, regional or national organisations. Where researchers seek to develop inquiry in specific organisational contexts, gaining access to participants can be a challenge. Researchers who have some form of pre-existing relationship with the organisation are often at an advantage, and cultivating productive relationships with key people (gatekeepers) who can help negotiate access to others is often integral to success. Most organisations, however, will need to consider the ethical and legal implications of allowing access (Sanders and Wilkins, 2010); transparency about research is therefore integral to building trust and to enable organisations to make informed decisions about research engagement. Organisations invariably need to be persuaded of the value of the research to them and often allow entry on the basis of having copies of the research findings. However, this can create ethical problems in terms of participant confidentiality and anonymity, and for research validity, as researchers need to consider how their findings might be 'swayed' by the knowledge of who will read the final report.

Where larger research populations do exist, researchers need to consider carefully who should be included in the sample. It might be the case, for example, that a researcher rationalises the inclusion of semi-structured interviews for between three and five participants in a small-scale ideographic study on counsellors' experiences of changing supervisors. Problems may arise, however, if sixty willing participants respond to an advert placed in a professional periodical (admittedly this is perhaps unlikely). Population criteria and methods of sample selection need to be made explicit prior to the commencement of research, in such a way as to limit potential bias (McLeod, 2007a). Table 6.2 highlights some of the main ways in which researchers select samples from wider populations.

Most researchers, however, engage in convenience or 'opportunity' sampling. In this way, researchers involve participants who 'fit' the parameters of the research population (in the case of the example above, counsellors who have changed supervisors) on an opportune basis (often through 'snowballing' or word of mouth) until the required sample size has been met. 'Sampling' of this nature is the norm for most counselling practitioner-researchers, but risks significant bias as it is unlikely to be representative of the wider research population. For this reason, some commentators suggest that it is, in fact, a form of 'non-sampling'.

Sampling method	Explanation
Random sampling	Pulling names or corresponding numbers 'out of a hat' – each potential participant has the same statistical chance of being selected.
Systematic sampling	Participants are selected randomly through systematic means. Using the example above (counsellors changing supervisors) the sixty people in the research population are ordered by length of therapeutic experience. A maximum of five participants is required, so a number between one and twelve (population size (60) divided by required sample size (5)) is randomly selected. This turns out to be the number 4, thereafter every twelfth person is chosen, meaning that numbers 4, 17, 29, 41 and 53 are the sample. The advantage here is that a breadth of therapeutic experience can be included in the research.
Stratified sampling	Here, particular information regarding the research population is required prior to sampling. This might include age, gender, length of experience, number of clinical hours a therapist has experience of, therapeutic orientation, etc. Each of these categories is considered a stratum. The researcher might be interested in developing a research sample that is statistically representative of the overall research population based on primary therapeutic orientation. Using the information provided on this stratum, he or she will randomly select a sample that proportionally reflects the principal therapeutic orientations of the overall population.

Table 6.2: Sampling methods (after Sanders and Wilkins, 2010)

Good planning should also allow for pilot studies, which help to avoid unnecessary pitfalls and the repetition of errors. In piloting, the researcher is able to ascertain whether the research instrument is suitable for generating the type of data that is anticipated. Pilot studies therefore enable research questions (and how they are asked in the case of interviews) to be reordered and refined. Researchers must decide and make explicit whether to utilise willing colleagues who are not part of the main sample (and who may not have direct experience of the phenomenon under investigation) to gauge the effectiveness of data collection methods, or to use and include initial data from the main study prior to its iteration (Atkins and Wallace, 2010). Pilot testing not only allows the researcher to make his or her own formative interpretative judgements concerning the potential veracity of the study, it also provides a platform for feedback from pilot participants regarding the structure, clarity and general experience of their participation.

THINKING ABOUT ETHICS

The subject of ethics is vast. Philosophers and ethicists have argued for millennia about its nature. Yet, in considering research we are required to focus our thinking firmly on ideas of morality and virtue to ensure that our research practices are aligned with both our personal values as people, and our professional values as therapists. Ethics are therefore a matter of integrity. They are enshrined in our value bases (Farrimond, 2012) and consciously and unconsciously inform our behaviours. However, perhaps more than most, the process of undertaking research calls us to examine ethical ideas, and make our thinking and actions explicit. Ethical practice in therapy and research needs to go beyond mechanistic considerations of 'applying' particular codes, or 'passing' the requirements of university ethics committees; it asks us to consider critically something of our roots, of our very being.

Ethical principles are just that – principles. They need to be contextualised by practitioner-researchers and those who advise them in order to 'test' the appropriateness of research practices. Ethical ideas can help us to consider and manage our behaviours and practices. Ethics are enshrined in Aristotle's idea of 'the good life'. Such a notion is, of course, subjective and open to varying interpretations that are dependent on the context in which it is framed. Doing what is 'right' in the processes of generating knowledge for wider benefit needs to be balanced against any potential harm to co-researchers. Some topics (for example, researching the experiences of client-survivors of childhood abuse) may more obviously cause co-contributors to re-experience difficult and painful emotions and sensations; yet seemingly more innocuous research topics might equally lead co-contributors to discuss or re-experience difficult or untapped events (Guillemin and Gillam, 2004). As an extreme, we might argue that, on the basis of *potential* harm, no research whatever should be conducted. This, however, would result in no new knowledge being generated, a position that is equally undesirable, as research is premised on the ethical basis of contributing knowledge that advances understanding and human well-being.

As we have argued elsewhere in this text, practitioner research, like therapy, involves us in relationship with others. It often utilises ways of being and skills sets that we embody in practice. Such relationships require us to consider values and the ethical principles they inform, and to deliberate the similarities and distinctions of those relationships and the ethical principles that support them. Hanley et al. (2013) argue that ethical ideals are intangible, and ask us to examine ways in which ethics are 'grounded' within clinical practice. In doing so, we might think about how we treat clients with 'respect', we try to do our best for them, we try to treat them fairly, we avoid therapeutic interventions that we *know* are inappropriate or may cause harm, and we are accountable through belonging and adhering to the requirements of a professional organisation, by discussing clinical work in supervision, and by attending to our personal and professional development. Ethically boundaried practice matters; it enables therapists to develop rich, creative, expansive yet safe spaces for clients to explore, find, feel, heal, conclude and be.

REFLECTION POINT

• How do you foster ethical practice in client work?
• What is the impact of doing so?

Different ethical positions are possible. Each offers us something, yet each on its own is limited and potentially problematic. Table 6.3 considers the key thinking of some ethical positions developed by famous ethicists and ethical 'schools'.

Ethicist/ethical 'school'	Key idea	Limitations
Immanuel Kant (1724–1804)	'I behave in this way, because this behaviour is universal.' Kant argued that our actions and behaviours should be consistent irrespective of context; that doing good or the right thing should be the imperative whether that is in our private, public or professional lives.	Needs and contexts inform the application of ethical principles and practices.
Utilitarian	Ensure you do the greatest good and promote the greatest happiness for the greatest number of people.	This position marginalises the minority. Those with power in a given situation have their voices heard and rights upheld most.
John Rawls (1921–2002) (see Rawls, 1971)	Rights are embodied in the individual rather than collectively; the individual matters most. We build a fair, ethical and mutually respectful society where everyone can 'be' and express themselves freely.	Potentially justifies views and actions that the majority may find abhorrent.

Table 6.3: Ethicists and ethical 'schools' – key thinking (after Roberts, 2009)

ACTIVITY 6.3

Look at Table 6.3. Which ethical ideas inform:

- your own values?
- your clinical practice?
- the ethical framework of the professional body to which you belong?

Ethical considerations are at the heart of research design and implementation; they are *the moral principles that guide activity from inception to completion* (Smith, 2010, p41). This is especially the case when people act as co-contributors in research, and more so when considering potentially sensitive topics that occur within the therapeutic system. Too often, however, ethical principles can feel restrictive. They can be experienced more like a list of 'thou shalt nots', which attempt to sanitise work, rather than provide a framework that promotes the freedom to practise and research within defined spaces.

In this vein, Proctor and Keys argue:

> *Ethics is a fluid internalised and vital part of our everyday lives, where the personal and professional are intertwined. It is about how we act in the world on the basis of what we value and believe.*
>
> (2013, p422)

Therefore, rather than being viewed as a set of rules, ethical principles should help generate creative practices and enable responsive and intuitive ways of being with ourselves and others, and provide negotiated, collaborative frameworks for innovative risk-taking within flexible, yet safe parameters (Owens et al., 2012). Most research projects will require some form of ethical 'clearance', often from a university ethics committee. While recognising the need for pragmatic engagement with committee requirements, it is also important to think critically about some of the dominant discourses that underpin some committees' work (Halse and Honey, 2007).

Ethical thinking in research has been seized by the prevailing hegemonic discourses of positivist research, which are concerned with generating knowledge through experimental methodologies. As a result, much ethical thinking in research remains (unhelpfully) framed within scientific ideas, most notably by the field of bioethics (Connolly and Reid, 2007). These dominant positivist ideas seem to have been placed *carte blanche* on to the qualitative domain without due understanding or consideration of conceptual differences between ontologies and epistemologies, or of the contextual *relationships* that undergird much qualitatively informed research practice (Lincoln and Tierney, 2004; Macfarlane, 2010). In this way, many ethics committees are grounded in ideas of *accountability, risk-management and regulation [which] are terms from a culture where external standards, conformity and suspicion prevail over uniqueness, humaneness and trust* (Proctor and Keys, 2013, p423). Many students and researchers as a result find themselves having to comply with the often rigid requirements of ethics committees (which attempt to control illusionary variables), in order to gain clearance to proceed with their research. Despite the criticism of the deficit position adopted by many ethics committees, it is important to recognise that they act merely as agents of wider regulatory frameworks, and often have a genuine concern for the welfare of research participants, the researcher and the reputation of the institution. Ethics committees tend only to meet a few times a year, so ensuring that any required research proposals and ethical protocol documents are completed, checked and submitted in plenty of time is critical, in order that research is 'signed off' to enable research to proceed. Completing documentation can be a supportive mechanism to help us actively consider research design and ways in which potential ethical issues might be addressed. As such, preparatory procedural ethical processes like these should not be viewed as merely mechanistic, but as a tool for active learning (Farrimond, 2012). Ethical ideas and practices should permeate research; it is therefore inadequate for researchers to prepare for and gain 'ethical clearance' and think 'I've done the ethics bit now.' Ethics are integral to who we are as people and professionals; therefore, active and ongoing ethical reflection concerning the entire research process is required in order to ensure best care for others, self and the research.

Procedural ethics and ethical codes therefore provide us with a framework to help us *be* ethical and to think and research in an ethical way. They can help to engender an internal locus of accountability, and enable us to *articulate our ethics in a meaningful way to others* (Proctor and Keys, 2013, p423). Practice and research frameworks across many disciplines are underpinned by the common principles of beneficence (doing good), non-maleficence (doing no harm), justice (fairness), fidelity (honouring trust) and autonomy (enabling people to be heard and make their own decisions) (Bond, 2004, 2010; BACP, 2013; Ransome, 2013).

Ethics committees are likely to scrutinise research proposals against these principles, and it is therefore helpful to consider and explain ways in which proposed research fulfils these 'requirements'. Most ethics committees tend to approach submissions from a deficit position, and interrogate work on the basis of potential risks and harm, rather than the good that may arise. Pragmatism is required, and it is important for would-be researchers to consider their research proposals from the mind-set of the ethics committee to ensure that potential hurdles and objections are proactively addressed, and the mitigation of potential risks is clearly explained.

ACTIVITY 6.4

The mind map in Figure 6.1 outlines some of the key factors that most ethics committees will examine in considering a research proposal in which the identification and management of potential risks are centrally cast.

- Using the ethical principles of beneficence, non-maleficence, justice, fidelity and autonomy as outlined above, evaluate with others any risks that an ethics committee might identify with your research proposal.
- How will you address and proactively mitigate these risks?

Trust is central to the relationship between therapist and client, and the processes that occur between researcher and participant. Social research is often framed in a particular type of relationship between participant and researcher. As such, researchers must pay due attention to that relationship and ensure that participants are not unduly exposed to different forms of risk that research has the capacity to generate. In this way, the counselling practitioner-researcher needs to ensure ongoing awareness of processes that may occur within the research relationship and take sufficient account of the contextual features that are unique to each research endeavour (i.e. topic, participants, methodology, data collection methods etc.). Bond notes that:

> . . . in research that requires an extended relationship between researcher and participants and/or the disclosure of personally sensitive issues, it is best practice to ensure that the researcher is supported by regular and on-going supervision, that is comparable to the ethical requirements for supervision in counselling and psychotherapy.
>
> (2004, p6)

The question of who will be involved in research is an essential consideration for the researcher and the ethics committee. Matters of vulnerability, power and the interrelationship between researcher and co-researcher are key ethical deliberations. While there may be a good rationale for asking clients about their experiences of therapy (if that is what we are investigating), their main preoccupation in therapy is therapy, which research engagement might detract from (or enhance).

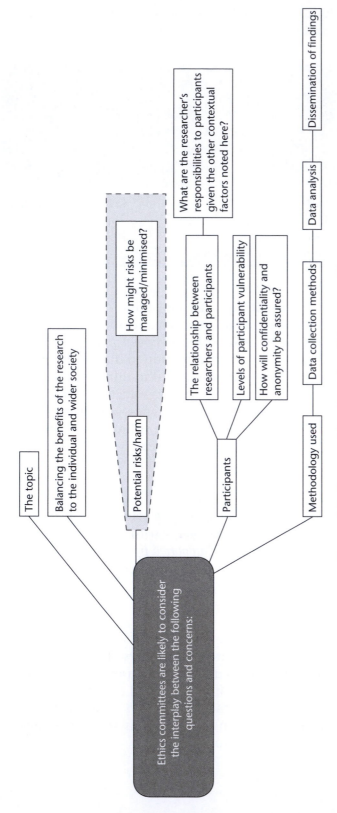

Figure 6.1: Key considerations for ethics committees

In this way:

> *. . . some might argue that a more ethical position is to talk to clients after therapy has terminated, although a differing opinion could question the ethics of revisiting and scratching away at a scab that has healed, without the support of psychological therapy.*
>
> (Hanley et al., 2013, p126)

Researchers, therefore, need to consider carefully who to involve in research and, in doing so, take account of the interplay between the nature of the topic, the methodology and potential relational dynamics that may exist between the researcher and participants. Given these factors, student-researchers sometimes elect to engage fellow counsellors as research participants. While this might not enable the voice of the client to be heard directly, it is often viewed as less ethically problematic. However, the researcher must also pay due care and attention to issues of positionality, duality and appropriate contracting when engaging fellow students or therapists as co-researchers.

Bond (2004) argues that trust between researcher and participant is integral to ethical research practice. It speaks of fidelity, fairness and integrity. Trust is the foundation of ethical research relationships; it places the onus on the researcher to be aware of and to manage the relational borderlands and dual processes that can exist between therapy and research. Such bonds of trust must be taken seriously by researchers; research relationships should help participants to make informed decisions (thereby enabling informed consent) about their participation. In this way, there must be:

- trust in the researcher's competence;
- trust in the researcher's ability to prioritise the welfare of participants over the 'requirements' of the research;
- trust in the researcher's respectful and fair treatment of participants;
- trust in the researcher's ability to treat personal experience with care and sensitivity;
- trust in the researcher's capacity to anonymise participants' identities and to ensure the secure protection of data;
- trust in the transparency of research processes by participants and readers in order to ensure the integrity and validity of the work; research should 'tell the truth', and not manipulate the participant's experiential voice;
- trust that the researcher will promote the participant's autonomous voice, including his or her fundamental right to amend or withdraw their participation at any time;
- transparency about the processes involved in the research and its potential dissemination.

Additional consideration needs to be given when undertaking research with cohorts deemed particularly vulnerable (including people in secure accommodation or prison, those experiencing cognitive decline or learning difficulties, and children and young people under the age of 16). In these instances, when it is deemed appropriate to proceed with research, it is often necessary to gain additional consent by proxy from others (e.g. parents, carers, professionals) who can act on behalf of participants. More recently, advances in children's rights have led to changes in ethical protocols concerning children's participation in research. Children and young people are increasingly seen as competent social actors (Kellett, 2010; Corsaro, 2011), who should be consulted on all matters concerning them (Jones and Welch, 2010). This right extends to children and young people making free and informed decisions about their participation in research. It is incumbent on any researcher to ensure that children and young people understand what the research is about and their right to opt in and out as they choose.

Therefore, the language used in and about research needs to be pitched at appropriate levels in order that children and young people can make appropriately informed decisions about their participation. Best research practice should therefore gain informed consent from the child or young person and an adult with parental or care responsibilities for the child, unless the young person is competent and able to consent fully on his or her own behalf in line with the Fraser Guidelines (NSPCC, 2012). In this way, Heath et al. note:

> the seeking of parental consent is often viewed as a necessary complement to an under-16 year old's own consent – and in some institutional settings may even be extended to young people *over* the age of 16.
> (2009, p29; emphasis in original)

Practitioner-researchers must be ethically mindful. They need to anticipate and engage proactively with ethical issues. The welfare of participants is integral, and researchers should make appropriate arrangements to signpost participants towards ongoing support, supervision or further therapy should the research leave participants feeling vulnerable in any way. With this in mind, it is often best to advise participants of the research topic, questions and processes in advance via written communication in order that they can make an informed decision about their participation. By attaching a form that is signed and returned, the researcher can maintain effective documentary evidence of each participant's informed consent.

As we have noted, the subject of ethics needs not only to be considered in theory, it requires the researcher to be continually alive to what is happening in the research field, and carefully and judiciously to apply ethical principles in all they do in order to ensure the well-being of others and the integrity of both researcher and research.

CHAPTER SUMMARY

Research can be an enriching but nonetheless challenging activity. For many counselling practitioner-researchers it becomes an all-consuming experience that dominates the landscape of their lives for a relatively short, but intense, period. In this chapter, we have considered how good planning, which is alive to possibilities and pitfalls, can enable research to run more smoothly. We have also revisited ethics as a site of personal and professional integrity, and anticipated ways in which ethical ideals become integrated with research processes, while offering some critical evaluation of procedural frameworks and how these might be pragmatically navigated.

SUGGESTED FURTHER READING

Bond, T (2004) *Ethical Guidelines for Researching Counselling and Psychotherapy*. Lutterworth: British Association for Counselling and Psychotherapy. Available at www.bacp.co.uk/research/ethical_guidelines. php

An excellent, succinct set of guidelines that is a must read for all counsellors undertaking research.

Farrimond, H (2012) *Doing Ethical Research*. Basingstoke: Palgrave Macmillan.

An accessible, but thorough, introduction to research ethics.

CHAPTER 7

What others have said: doing a literature review

John AJ Dixon

CORE KNOWLEDGE

By the end of this chapter, you will be able to:

- explain the purpose of a literature review as part of an academic research project;
- identify the stages involved in conducting a literature review;
- conduct a literature review.

This chapter aims to provide practical advice and suggestions on conducting a literature review. It starts by making some assumptions; first, that you are undertaking a course of study that requires the completion of a major research project; and second, that your research involves the collection and analysis of primary data. As a general point the process of conducting a literature review is something that cannot be rushed; it is time-consuming, but can provide you with a solid grounding in understanding your topic, and can be thoroughly rewarding and enriching.

WHAT IS THE PURPOSE OF A LITERATURE REVIEW?

Conducting a literature review is a way of getting a sense of the wider context of your own research topic. It is likely that, when developing a research idea, you begin to think about an area of interest; you may have already defined a specific research question, and have begun to engage with literature on your chosen topic.

ACTIVITY 7.1

- Make a list of the current sources of information you have used in defining your research interest and developing your research question.
- Now, divide the list into the following:
  - textbooks;
  - websites;
  - popular media (newspapers, magazines, television);
  - research papers and academic journals;
  - systematic reviews.
- Identify the potential advantages and disadvantages of each of these sources of information.
- Which sources of information are you drawing on most?

Spending some time thinking about the sources that inform your understanding of a topic is important when conducting research. A literature review should attempt to draw on academically robust sources to support your understanding of a subject. Generally speaking, when conducting research there is an expectation that the wider research literature (specifically research papers and academic journals) will inform the majority of your understanding of a topic. While other sources may provide relevant information, there may be issues regarding their currency and reliability. A textbook, for example, is likely to summarise the key issues relevant to a given topic, but might only provide an overview and act as a stimulus for further reading. Websites can be published by anyone and therefore need to be scrutinised; authors' credentials and biases need to be checked. It is likely that completing Activity 7.1 has highlighted some of these issues. That is not to say, however, that research papers and academic journals are not without their problems, but generally we can be assured that published research has been through a rigorous process of peer review, and has been produced following recognised methodological reference points that can be checked and scrutinised.

A literature review serves a number of purposes; Ridley (2012) argues that a literature review enables students to engage with, synthesise and convey understanding of the historical background, contemporary contexts, theoretical underpinnings and terminological bases of the topic. While it is a task that is time-consuming and requires considerable thought and effort, it can actually save researchers unnecessary effort in conducting their own research. Getting acquainted with the literature on a topic assists in identifying gaps in knowledge about the subject as well as highlighting what has already been covered, which questions have been asked and which questions remain. If your research project is asking a question that has been asked by other researchers, you might consider whether asking the same question again is worthwhile, what it will add to the existing knowledge base and whether a different approach to the question might be better applied. It is likely that the answers to these points will only begin to reveal themselves through the process of acquainting oneself with what is already 'known', thereby creating opportunities to build upon this knowledge base.

The process of reviewing literature can be thought of as engaging in a dialogue with others who have explored the subject of your research before; you may find yourself debating the ideas presented and grappling with competing points of view. As we engage with the literature, we learn who the key thinkers are and the direction research has been moving in. Embarking on research is a process of learning and you should not be afraid to contact established researchers in your subject area for information, pointers or suggestions; it is likely you will discover that they are interested in what you are doing and may want to know about the outcomes of your project. In this sense, reviewing literature can be viewed as a means of building professional networks and relationships as well as engaging in critical debate about the subject being studied.

Oliver offers a useful rationale for conducting a literature review:

> . . . *when you are researching a topic, it usually has to be fairly narrow and focused, and because of this it can be difficult to appreciate how your research subject is connected to other related areas. The overall purpose of a literature review is to demonstrate this, and to help the reader understand how your study fits into a broader context.*
>
> (2012, p5)

This quotation raises a number of interesting issues for the student conducting a research project. Usually you will be subject to pretty tight time constraints and you may find yourself torn between wanting to investigate fully your research topic and the temptation to get swept away and diverted into interesting but not specifically relevant areas. The challenge in reviewing literature is selecting sources that are relevant to your research topic while engaging with wider issues relevant to the context of the research question. Bowers-Brown and Stevens (2010) make the point that an attempt to review all of the literature on a subject is almost impossible due to issues of availability, accessibility and the time available in which to conduct the review. As a result, the researcher needs to prioritise and set parameters for what should and should not be included.

HOW DO I BEGIN? (WHAT LITERATURE?)

It is useful to begin the literature review with the following points in mind. The review should not be a descriptive list summarising all the information you have found about the topic under investigation. Instead, a good review will offer analytical and critical discussion of the literature, focusing on each individual source and on the wider body of research available (Jesson et al., 2012), and should therefore be defined by the research question.

It might be helpful at this point if you have an idea about the main themes you wish to explore in your research and have begun to refine your research question. Having this established makes it easier to begin the literature review as you already have some sense of what you want to explore.

This is a useful activity and highlights some important considerations that will form the basis of starting the search for relevant literature. If you have a well-defined research question, the process of beginning a literature search is likely to be simpler. What is important is that you begin to have an idea of the sort of information you need to look for.

For example: you may be interested in the experience of same-sex couples accessing counselling for relationship issues. This is not quite a research aim or question as yet but provides sufficient ideas on which to begin a search. A quick brainstorm is likely to identify a range of topics that may or may not be relevant to what you want to investigate; what is important at this stage is the identification of potentially related issues.

Figure 7.1 provides an illustration of some of the issues that may be linked to the researcher's area of interest. When you have an extensive list you can begin the process of refining what you are actually interested in and begin searching for literature.

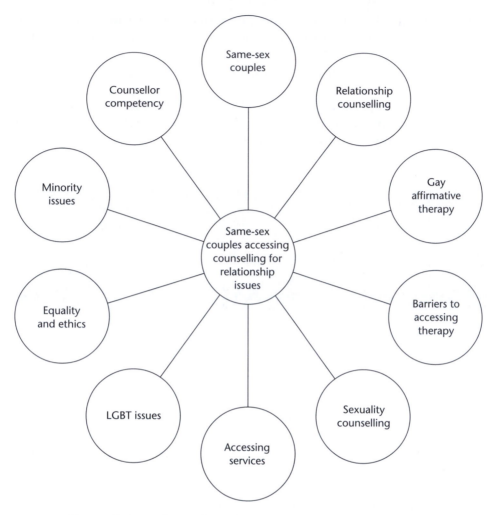

Figure 7.1: Key issues linked to a researcher's area of interest

If you are uncertain, select a few areas that stand out for you and begin searching for relevant literature. Reading around your topic of interest can provide a means of refining your research question; this allows the researcher to become more familiar with what is known, what the issues are, and where gaps remain in the current literature. Remember, you need to refine your research interest into a succinct research aim/question. For further advice, read Chapter 4.

SEARCHING FOR LITERATURE

Conducting a literature search can be complicated; however, the modern researcher has the significant advantage of having access to published research online via various databases. Imagine living in a world with no internet and trying to find as much information as you can about your topic of interest! It is likely that you would have to travel great distances and spend vast amounts of time and money to get all the information you needed.

FINDING SOURCES

Davis et al. offer some useful advice for nursing students conducting literature searches:

> *When you want to find the best sources of evidence to support your studies and practice, you need to engage thoughtfully and thoroughly in searching within the databases available to you.*
>
> (2011, p142)

A literature search is simply the process of looking for sources of information. We have already established that research papers, systematic reviews and journals are generally considered to be the best sources of supporting literature for a research project, but how do we begin to find the most appropriate literature? Aveyard (2010) advocates a systematic approach to the literature search to ensure thoroughness and engagement with as broad a literature base as possible. Some practical suggestions include:

- consideration of the types of literature you wish to include in your search (textbooks, journal articles, research papers);
- establishing the key words, phrases or terms that are most relevant to your research aim/question;
- setting inclusion and exclusion criteria for your search.

ACTIVITY 7.4

Step 1. Write down your research question and underline or highlight the key issues being explored by listing the key words. For example, your research question that has developed from Activity 7.3 might be something like this:

'How do *couple counsellors* perceive *relationship issues* presented by *same-sex couples* compared to the issues presented by *heterosexual couples*?'

The key terms/words associated with this research question are in italic.

Step 2. Make a note of any words that might be associated with these key terms, including synonyms. These will eventually act as the basis for starting your literature search.

For example, the table below identifies some possible key terms/words associated with the research question as well as some related issues.

Couple counsellors/ counselling	Relationship issues	Same-sex and same-sex couples	Couples	Heterosexual and heterosexual couples
Relationship therapists	Conflict	Lesbian	Relationship	Hetero-normative
Relate counselling	Sexuality	Gay	Partners	Straight
Relationship counselling	Intimacy	Bisexuality	Loving	Marriage
Couple psychotherapists/ psychotherapy	Attachment	Sexual minorities	Boyfriend/ girlfriend	
Marriage guidance	Infidelity	Civil partnerships		
Relationship support	Affairs Separation Divorce	Gay marriage Homosexuality		

It is useful to remember that terminology and language changes over time, and that different cultures may use different terms. The spelling of words also varies; an obvious example is the English (UK) term 'counsellor' and English (US) term 'counselor'; being mindful of these spelling variations can assist in broadening your literature search.

Step 3. Identify the academic journals and databases your academic institution subscribes to by speaking to your tutor or institution's librarians. Librarians are an invaluable, but often underused, student resource; they have expert knowledge of the institution's library stock, in both electronic and print formats.

BEGINNING THE SEARCH

Now that you have a list of key terms you are ready to begin seeking out literature. The most straightforward and fastest way of conducting a literature search is through the use of electronic databases. Your academic institution will be able to advise you on which databases it has access to; these usually contain a vast wealth of source materials that are not available through other internet-based search engines, for example 'Google Scholar'. This is not to say that search engines do not have a place in a literature search; however, you are unlikely to find the wealth of material you need by relying solely on a free internet search engine (Davis et al., 2011).

To commence your review, you need to consider where you are likely to find the best sources of information. There are a number of electronic databases devoted to specific subject areas that may be of use as a starting place, but ultimately it will be a matter of what you have access to through your academic institution. Do not limit yourself to a single database; instead use your search terms in a number of different databases to maximise your results.

ACTIVITY 7.5

- As a means of getting started, begin a literature search using 'Google Scholar' to explore how different combinations of search terms yield different results. Commence with key terms that feature in your research question and then try alternating key words and terms using the list you made in Activity 7.4.

Aveyard (2010) suggests starting with an advanced search; this is a useful idea, as simply typing in your whole research question into the search box is likely to return lots of irrelevant results. Remember, you are trying to find the most useful sources of information relevant to your research topic, and you should ensure that your literature search is guided by your research aim/question. See Figure 7.2.

You have probably noticed from conducting this search that you get a lot of results; however, not all will be relevant to your research topic and you will need to consider how to refine your search further. This is where 'inclusion' and 'exclusion' criteria are useful. The purpose of setting out these criteria is to ensure that your research is consistently guided by your research question. Aveyard argues:

> *Clear and well-defined inclusion and exclusion criteria will ensure that you do not get side-tracked with the data (literature) that are not strictly relevant to your review. Thus, setting appropriate criteria assists you in keeping your study focused.*

> (2010, p71)

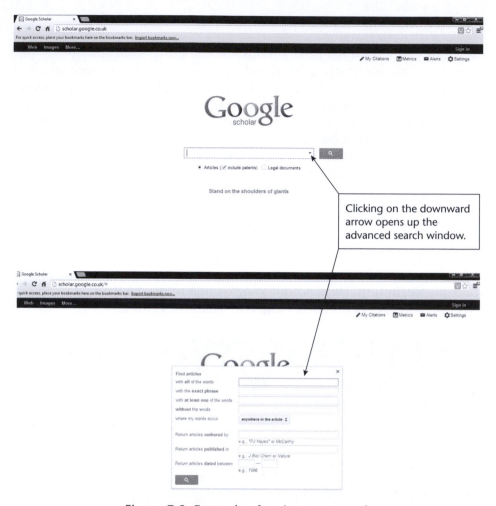

Figure 7.2: Example of an internet search

These criteria must ultimately be guided by your research question and you will need to consider what information is going to be most useful or relevant to answering your question. Oliver quite rightly points out that *the writing of a literature review is a creative activity* (2012, p59); it is therefore difficult to provide exact pointers about what should or should not be included. However, by means of example, the following could be seen as *possible* inclusion and exclusion criteria.

Inclusion criteria might comprise:

- peer-reviewed journal articles;
- works published in the last ten years;
- seminal works on the research topic;
- works cited frequently by other research in the same discipline.

Exclusion criteria might comprise:

- works that have not been peer reviewed;
- works that have not included primary research.

It is essential in defining 'inclusion' and 'exclusion' criteria that you can justify your decisions so that the reader understands your rationale; this requires some thought and needs to be based on objective, rational judgements, and often pragmatic decisions about the scope of your literature review. Ultimately, the criteria you establish will be unique to your review, and you may not be able to define these criteria straight away until you have begun searching for and reading the literature in order to get a better sense of your research topic and the issues that are relevant to your research question.

DEVELOPING YOUR SEARCH

You may have found from your search using 'Google Scholar' that you were unable to access all of the material returned without logging into a website or paying for an article. General internet search engines can be a good starting point to 'test the ground' for information in the public domain. However, to access specific academic sources and broaden your search you cannot rely solely on search engines; the use of academic and subject-specific databases is essential. Your academic institution will have access to specialist academic journals through electronic databases that are not available to the general public, but which as a student you will be able to access. Some examples might include:

- the Cochrane Library – systematic reviews useful to health and social care professionals;
- PsychINFO – abstracts for journal articles in psychology;
- Scopus – articles from a range of different subject areas;
- CINAHL (Cumulative Index to Nursing and Allied Health Literature) – journal articles relevant to nursing and allied health professionals.

The list above is by no means exhaustive, but gives an indication regarding the sorts of possible databases that your institution may have access to and which should be made good use of when conducting your literature search (Aveyard, 2010; Davis et al., 2011).

When conducting a search using an academic database the concept of *Boolean logic* is useful; it can extend your literature search by organising key terms or related ideas in conducting different types of search. The method relies on Boolean operators, which allow you to either broaden or narrow a search (Davis et al., 2011). In simple terms, using the words 'OR, AND, NOT' in searches provides instructions to the database search engine to either include or exclude certain information in the results it returns. This probably sounds complicated but consider the following examples (adapted from Davis et al., 2011; Oliver, 2012).

- Searching for the term **counselling** alone is likely to yield many results that may not be relevant to your research question. If you searched for **counselling OR psychotherapy** the search will return results that include either term. This broadens your search to include any of the search terms you define.
- Alternatively, you could try **counselling AND psychotherapy**. In this case your search is narrowed to only include results that include both terms. This could be especially useful if you are trying to locate something specific, for example **counselling AND couples AND LGBT**; in this case only results that include all three search terms will be returned.
- If you want to exclude something from your search you could employ the word 'NOT', for example **counselling NOT psychotherapy**. In this case only results that mention counselling and not psychotherapy would be returned.

You can use this idea to develop complex search patterns that include and exclude search terms by applying brackets in your searches.

- Searching for the term **counselling AND (couples NOT families)** will include all papers that mention counselling and couples but exclude those that mention families. As a general rule the search engine would deal with what is in the brackets first before then searching for sources including the terms outside the brackets.
- Searching for **(counselling OR psychotherapy) AND couples** will include all papers that mention counselling or psychotherapy and couples.
- Searching for **(counselling OR psychotherapy) AND (couples OR families)** would return papers that potentially discuss counselling couples, counselling families, psychotherapy and couples, psychotherapy and families.

Tips

1. It is important to keep track of your literature searches so that you can refer to them later; you may also need to provide some explanation when you write up your review about how you found particular sources. Keeping track at this point saves time later.
2. Keep a reference list of all the papers you identify in your searches that are relevant to your research topic. It can cause a great deal of

heartache to know you found a really useful paper but cannot remember where, or who it was by.

OTHER SOURCES OF LITERATURE

Other methods for conducting a literature search include searching reference lists of published papers for additional source materials. Each journal article will provide pointers to other key literature that informed the author's thinking; spending some time searching through the reference list is likely to highlight papers you may want to find yourself to support your research. In addition you may begin to notice patterns in the papers you read; perhaps the same authors are cited in multiple papers on your topic of interest. This can be extremely useful and can act as a basis for a literature search using the authors' details.

Some electronic databases have a 'cited by' function, which finds sources that have cited the article you have identified since its publication. This function is especially useful to track how the source has been used and how the topic has developed.

Your literature search may reveal that many of the sources you identify are from the same journal publication. If this is the case, you may want to do a focused search on that journal; if your academic institution holds print copies, you could conduct a manual search. This can be time-consuming, but may reveal articles that might not be found in electronic databases (Aveyard, 2010; Oliver, 2012).

A note on interlibrary loans

While academic institutions have access to an extensive range of literature, occasionally you may identify articles that you would like to read from journals to which your institution has not subscribed. If this is the case, you might speak to your librarian about *interlibrary loans*, which allow you to access papers from other institutions.

ACTIVITY 7.6

By this point, you may have collected a number of research papers relevant to your research question. Spend some time thinking about how you might group the papers together. The following questions may be helpful.

- Who authored the paper and what were they setting out to do?
- Are the authors prominent writers in the field or new researchers?
- What theoretical perspective is informing the research?
- How many participants were involved in the research? What was the methodology used?
- What were the key findings, conclusions or recommendations?
- What were the strengths and limitations of the paper? How does the paper relate to others collected on the topic?
- How does the paper relate to your research question?

After you have read several papers consider the following.

- What are the common threads or themes running through them?
- Are there methodological similarities or differences?
- What are the key debates, areas of contention, and areas of agreement?
- What are the research gaps?
- How do the papers represent the development of the topic?
- How does your research fit with these?

WHAT TO DO WHEN YOU HAVE YOUR SOURCE MATERIAL – WRITING UP THE REVIEW

A common question that many students ask is: 'At what point should I start writing up my literature review?' This is not an easy question to answer, as you may not know when you have all of the information you need to include in the review. The size of your review may also determine at which point you decide to begin your write-up. In a dissertation of 10,000 words you might devote 2,000–3,000 to your literature review. It can be useful to begin the review and maintain it as an evolving draft until you have finished your research project. However, you cannot begin your review until you have first read a substantial amount of the literature you have found on your topic.

> *A good literature review does not simply choose literature, divide it into sections and then describe it. It does all these things, but much more besides.*
> (Oliver, 2012, p75)

ACTIVITY 7.7

- Reread the first section of this chapter on 'What is the purpose of a literature review?' and make notes on the key points that should be addressed. This will help you to shape your review chapter.

A literature review chapter can be structured in a variety of ways, and to some extent should be guided by the expectations of your academic tutors or research supervisor. However, there are some points you may want to bear in mind when structuring your review. A good literature review chapter will have an introduction, a middle and a conclusion; writing the review, however, is not as simple as putting in these three subheadings and filling in the gaps. The review needs a clear structure that clearly sets out the following to the reader:

- how you conducted your literature search;
- your inclusion and exclusion criteria;
- the key literature you identified, and its scope and relevance to the topic under investigation;
- the current debates in relation to the topic;
- the current gaps in the research;
- where your research is positioned in terms of current debates and research gaps.

The introduction

Your 'introduction' should set the scene for your literature review, invite the reader into the broader topic area and identify key concerns. You should set out how you plan to discuss the issues by explaining what has been included (and excluded), and rationalise how the review is organised. It is important that the reader has some sense of how you went about collecting the literature that underpins your review. There is a need for some thought here; will the review be structured chronologically, or will it perhaps adopt a particular theoretical perspective? It is important that the reader understands the structure of the review; this might be explicitly stated, or indicated, through the use of subheadings in order to highlight the key issues or themes being addressed. However you choose to structure the review, you need to keep in mind that the reader needs to understand your thinking.

If a chronological approach is adopted, it would make sense to begin by examining early works on the topic, before drawing the reader's attention to subsequent papers; this enables discussion of changes in theory and practice over time. To do this, you need to consider what the literature has been saying, and to begin to group it appropriately.

If your review is adopting a particular theoretical perspective, it is important that you acknowledge different perspectives on the topic and provide a rationale for the theoretical perspective you adopt. For example, if you are discussing the issue of self-disclosure from a psychodynamic perspective, you could also discuss humanistic and cognitive behavioural standpoints and include research findings from these modalities. This demonstrates to the reader that you have a good understanding of the topic from a range of perspectives as well as offering some explanation of your adopted research approach.

The middle

As you move into the main body of your review, you should explore in some detail the issues you have uncovered. Try to avoid providing a description of one paper after another, such as 'Author A found this, but author B found that.' This is a tricky task as you need to convey to the reader something about each piece of literature that is part of the review. It is acceptable to focus on particular papers that seem most relevant to your research aims, but you should still try to articulate engagement with the wider topic. The reader needs to understand whether you are discussing a book, a research paper or another piece of source material. If you are discussing a research paper, the reader needs to get a sense of the author's aims and methodology together with the key findings in each paper discussed. If discussing textbooks or other secondary source materials, it is important that this is communicated to the reader. A good review will principally generate critical discussion by drawing upon the findings of a range of primary sources (original research pieces), while utilising secondary sources where appropriate.

> *One of the main purposes of a literature review is that you demonstrate your capacity to analyse and evaluate the writing of others.*
> (Oliver, 2012, p128)

It can be useful to consider grouping literature by themes, findings, or complementary or opposing viewpoints. You will not be able to address every point raised in every source you have read, but you do need to be able to engage in critical discussion that offers some synthesis of the presented ideas. Synthesis requires you to say something about what is emerging from the papers you have read about a topic. While each author in your review will make his or her own contribution to the topic under investigation, synthesis attempts to draw together the perspectives of multiple authors and offers an integrated interpretation of multiple information sources (Aveyard, 2010). This can only be successfully achieved by thoroughly engaging with each piece of source material. Activity 7.6 offered some questions you might consider using in order to begin critical engagement, and which may help form the basis of generating synthesised discussion. Remember, your aim here is to demonstrate your understanding of the relationship between the research question you are asking and the wider research topic; therefore, as you write the review you should move from critical engagement with the wider topic to identifying gaps in current research.

Concluding the review

A number of things need to be achieved to draw the literature review to a successful conclusion. A literature review is not a stand-alone piece of work; it needs to be linked to the rest of your research project (Aveyard, 2010; Davis et al., 2011; Oliver, 2012). Your concluding comments provide a means to sum up and draw together the literature presented in the review and state your own research position. Consider the following points.

- What are the major contributions that the reviewed literature makes to the topic?
- What is the current position of the topic area in relation to theory and its relevance to practice?
- What are the key gaps in current research; what questions remain?
- What might constitute relevant issues for future study?
- What is your research project seeking to do?

Addressing these questions in your concluding comments clearly contextualises your study within the wider subject knowledge base, and provides the reader with a sound insight into what has influenced your thinking. Moreover, the theoretical stance you have adopted, and any pre-existing assumptions you hold, are likely to be made clearer through your engagement with the literature. Your concluding comments are an opportunity to convey these assumptions within the context of the reviewed literature, thereby identifying any biases that may influence the outcome of the research project.

CHAPTER SUMMARY

This chapter has discussed the rationale for engaging with the literature as part of a research project. It has discussed reviewing the literature as a means of generating a critical backdrop for the work, and provided an overview of the processes involved in generating balanced and synthesised critique. This enables both researcher and reader to understand what has informed the positions adopted within the research, thereby enhancing reflexivity and transparency.

SUGGESTED FURTHER READING

Aveyard, H (2010) *Doing a Literature Review in Health and Social Care.* Milton Keynes: Open University Press.

An excellent and easy-to-read text aimed at health students, but full of useful information for students of other disciplines. It includes many helpful practical examples and exercises.

Oliver, P (2012) *Succeeding With Your Literature Review: A handbook for students.* Milton Keynes: Open University Press.

Another excellent and highly readable text, full of useful and practical suggestions.

CHAPTER 8

Making it happen: applying research methods

Graham Bright, Norman Claringbull and Gill Harrison

CORE KNOWLEDGE

By the end of this chapter, you will be able to:

- justify and apply research methodologies to counselling research;
- evaluate the application of research methodologies, and make proposals for their improvement.

We intend this as a practical chapter to enable readers to develop the confidence to apply research methodologies to their own work. Given the array of research approaches available, and the scope of what is reasonably achievable here, we have decided to focus on the application of two methodologies in order to offer readers templates that they can apply to their own research practice. First, we shall examine the application of Interpretative Phenomenological Analysis (IPA), a qualitative approach introduced in Chapter 5 (see pages 91–3), before moving on to an examination of quantitative methodologies.

INTERPRETATIVE PHENOMENOLOGICAL ANALYSIS

Our choice of IPA in this first part of the chapter is informed by a range of factors that we seek to make transparent. First, IPA holds lived experience as fundamental, while maintaining a commitment to locate and interpret experience within wider social constructs (Reid et al., 2005). In this way, IPA enables participant voices to be heard and deeply understood within constructed ideographies (Larkin et al., 2006). Such phenomenological and interpreted narrations of life events enable IPA to bricolage with other narrative approaches to facilitate the articulation of biographies, which are the fuel of the postmodern project that each of us enacts, and through which we generate meaning. As therapists and tutors who embrace therapeutic pluralism (Cooper and McLeod, 2011), yet who remain grounded in a humanistic axiology that values the phenomenological reality of each individual, and who draw upon psychodynamic models of interpretation, we recognise a particular alignment between our own values and IPA's axiological basis and dual ontology of phenomenology and interpretation. Second, many of our students have equally and naturally valued these positions, and have gained much from the rich data that their IPA studies have generated and the methodological framework that it provides. Finally, there is a demonstrable rise in the number of counselling studies that have utilised this approach; IPA is a methodology the counselling world appears to be increasingly willing to embrace.

Naturally, we recognise that researchers need to generate a clear rationale that aligns the topic under investigation with reflexive axiological and ontological positioning in justifying the use of particular methodological approaches. Therefore, we wish to make it clear that, despite our applied examination of IPA and quantification here, we value the appropriation of a range of methodologies as examined in Chapter 5 in aligning needs of different ontological positions within different types of study.

Here, however, we wish first to offer our vision of IPA as a flexibly applied methodology.

ACTIVITY 8.1

- Reread the section on IPA in Chapter 5 (see pages 91–3). As you read make a note of what is important and challenging.

In completing this task and on reflecting on the central tenets of IPA as outlined in Chapter 5, it is apparent that IPA holds sacrosanct the capacity of the researcher to be as close as possible to the lifeworld experiences of research participants in order to deeply understand phenomena from the other's perspective, while interpreting phenomenological essence within located ideographic contexts with which the researcher may have varying degrees of personal experience. Meaning and interpretation are fundamental. In approaching and generating a heuristically founded research question, it can be challenging for researchers to appreciate fully the very often personal experiences and biases that shape research formation, data gathering and analysis. Generating the capacity to take up a range of positions in relation to various research processes can be a helpful way of maintaining appropriate perspectives: reflexive awareness of where to self-position at various points is essential. Researchers who get and stay too close to the data for too long can end up distorting the picture, while not getting close enough often results in research that is dissonant and unrepresentative of participants' lived experiences. IPA demands ongoing researcher reflexivity in order to attune to phenomenological understanding of others' experiences and bring into awareness our own biases. Reflexivity is often a process best conducted with others, and the support of colleagues, supervisors, peers and tutors is helpful in fostering the transparent awareness that IPA requires.

Case study 8.1

Debbie worked within an agency that specialised in working with survivors of sexual violence. She was aware that a number of her clients had been diagnosed with a range of complex mental health issues, including dissociative identity disorder (DID), borderline personality disorder (BPD), psychosis and schizophrenia. The research question she formulated was:

Sexual violence counselling for women with complex mental health needs: What are the implications for the client–counsellor relationship?

Debbie undertook a qualitative study, carrying out semi-structured interviews with four counsellors, all of whom had experience of working with clients with a range of medically diagnosed complex mental health needs. Participants were provided with an interview schedule prior to the interviews. The following questions were included.

- What information did participants receive in referral documentation specifically related to diagnosis of complex mental health needs?
- What impact did this information have on the counsellor and the counselling relationship?
- How did supervision support the counsellor in working with clients with complex mental health needs?

The structure of the questions allowed participants to share their views of complex mental health needs. The researcher's own personal writings were weaved into the study producing autoethnographic data. All the data was analysed using IPA.

After analysing the data Debbie identified a number of themes; however, initially she was concerned about how they would be received as they challenged the very foundations of psychological practice. As a newly qualified counsellor Debbie felt ill-equipped to challenge recognised protocols for psychological diagnosis. Through supervision, personal reflection and a determination that her research might influence a change in attitude within her own agency, Debbie was able to communicate her in-depth analysis of the data with the authority it deserved. Her research came to the following conclusions.

- Participants perceived mental health services to be draconian, a system in which the client becomes lost; a system too big and too powerful to be challenged or changed.
- The labels/medical diagnoses used force professionals, the client and others to focus on that label rather than the cause of emotional distress.
- Despite such perceptions, participants battled to forge ways to collaborate with external services.
- Participants were aware of the need for self-care when working with sexual violence due to the subject matter; supervision was more than a professional necessity, it was an oasis, a crucial intervention to ensure emotional survival.
- The impact of unmet expectations of other services appeared to be outside participants' awareness.
- Each participant articulated strongly that working with a complex mental health need would not impact how he or she worked; however, upon further exploration each conceded there was a difference – the feeling of needing to put more into the therapeutic relationship.

Debbie's autoethnographic findings mirrored the feelings of her participants: injustice, anger, frustration and helplessness at not being able to influence a mental health system that abnormalises and pathologises a normal reaction to traumatic life events – factors that have ongoing implications for the therapeutic relationship. Participants were not only listening to clients working through the pain of their experiences, but had to contend with their own strong emotions born from the lack of awareness and acceptance shown to clients by other professionals. Participants also recognised the constraints of their own profession and clearly wanted a complete wrap-around service, but felt powerless to infiltrate an omnipotent statutory body. At all stages of analysis Debbie used her own reflections of working with clients and reflexivity in responding to participant data.

Debbie's study highlighted the inability of services to holistically meet the mental health needs of this client group. The recommendations strongly supported existing services to work differently and be jointly more client focused.

Reflexive engagement enabled Debbie to go beyond the cursory, to get closer to her own and others' experience. It helped her to overcome her initial anxiety about the data and tell the research story boldly in the way it merited. Debbie went on to present her research at a regional conference.

IPA provides a framework for knowing. Frameworks are useful structures that aid processes of construction, rather than rulebooks that require rigid adherence. The capacity to link rationalised research topics to a suitably constructed interview schedule is of real importance. Interview schedules should provide a framework to shape the direction of interviews, to ensure without recourse to rigidity that interviews with participants fulfil their intended purpose. For the purposes of IPA, structured interviews are considered too rigid, and while the more experienced researcher might successfully utilise an unstructured approach, for the most part semi-structured interviews are advised. Semi-structured interviews *represent a trade-off between consistency and flexibility* (Langdridge, 2007, p65), allowing researchers to detail the specific points they wish to cover, while creating scope for participants to tell their stories in 'surround sound'. Semi-structured interviews provide a framework for engagement and enable the development of trusting rapport between researcher and participant. As in therapy, rapport and trust in research are essential in enabling deeper experiential knowing and interpretative insight. The importance of participant confidence in, and ethical research practice by, the researcher cannot be overstated.

Smith et al. note:

> *The aim of developing a schedule is to facilitate a comfortable interaction with the participant which will, in turn, enable them to provide a detailed account of the experience under investigation. Questions should be prepared so that they are open and expansive; the participant should be encouraged to talk at length. Verbal input from the interviewer can be minimal.*
>
> (2009, p59)

The aim of an IPA interview is to enable participants to talk deeply about their experience of a given phenomenon and the meanings they attach to it. Interview schedules must be designed with this in mind. Questions should therefore be open, unambiguous, not leading, not overly empathic, and not manipulative.

Smith et al. suggest a range of typical questions prevalent in IPA interview schedules (see Table 8.1).

IPA interviews last between 45 and 90 minutes, and most typically around an hour. Between three and ten open questions with appropriate prompts provide an effective balance, enabling deep exploration while keeping conversation 'on track'. Many novice researchers tend towards employing more questions than necessary; however, overstructuring can stifle interviews and limit participant exploration. The process of developing an interview schedule is therefore a matter of iteration, which is often helped by trialling questions with peers and through insights gained from more formal pilot interviews. The interview schedule should reflect the scope and objectives of the overarching research question; care needs to be taken, however, to develop questions that participants can consider in a meaningful way. Researchers should make logical the order of their questions in order that they can be understood and considered in a coherent fashion.

Question	Example
Descriptive	What does counselling entail?
Narrative	Can you tell me why you became a therapist?
Structural	What are the processes involved in therapy from referral to completion?
Contrast	What for you are the main differences between successful and unsuccessful therapeutic outcomes?
Evaluative	How do you evaluate the effectiveness of what you do?
Circular	What does your clinical supervisor think about the organisation where you practice?
Comparative	How does being a counsellor compare to your previous employment?
Prompts	Can you tell me more about that, please?
Probes	What do you mean by 'challenging'?

Table 8.1: Questions in IPA interviews (after Smith et al., 2009, p60)

Furthermore, introductory questions should seek to elicit more descriptive and narrative responses in order that the researcher is able to contextualise participants' experiences. More gentle forms of questioning in the early stages of the interview enable the development of rapport, and prevent participants perceiving the research process as threatening – the result of which often leads to respondents 'clamming up'. It is important therefore to put participants at their ease. This process can sometimes be helped by supplying a copy of the interview schedule in advance; however, this can equally stunt the naturalness of the interview as participants then have time to pre-construct 'scripted' responses. In order to aid the naturalness of the interview process, researchers should seek to memorise questions, using the interview schedule as an aide-memoir to shape conversation if necessary.

Smith et al. therefore posit that the interview schedule should be used:

> . . . in a flexible manner. The schedule is a guide, which can incorporate ideas about how best to phrase the questions, and how best to move from general issues to more particular ones . . . Used effectively, and sensitively, semi-structured interviews can facilitate rapport and empathy, and permit great flexibility of coverage.
>
> (2009, pp64–6)

Counsellors have a natural advantage in this type of research as (albeit different forms of) interviews are integral to their professional daily lives. The importance of empathic listening in order to understand experience and meaning is at the heart of both therapy and IPA; a suitably constructed and open interview schedule therefore provides an appropriate foundation to enable each participant's phenomenological exploration to be understood, helping the researcher to have confidence in the interview, and the participant to have confidence in the researcher in facilitating the emergence of rich and engaging data.

It is best practice for those using IPA to inform participants about the broad scope of the topic, the relative openness of the agenda and the reason for the researcher's interest in the participant's contribution (ibid.). All of this can be explored at the commencement of the interview and contribute to the process of gaining the participant's informed consent, which should encompass confidentiality, anonymity and likely research processes and outputs. Research, like counselling, involves engaging in a particular type of relationship for a particular purpose. All relationships have at their core power imbalances. Relationships within the helping professions and research about the helping professions are ethically bound to recognise and minimise the effects of unhelpful power dynamics.

Those engaged in counselling research who employ methodologies such as IPA to elicit often deep phenomenological knowledge about delicate and complex personal and professional experiences need to recognise with sensitive ethical application the potential (if unintentional) abuses of power that can arise between researcher and participant. Gabriel (2009) has argued that researchers should value their relationships with contributors in the same fiduciary manner in which therapists honour what Bordin (1979) termed the *therapeutic alliance* of *bonds, tasks and goals*. Qualitative researchers should facilitate the creation of a safe space in which participants can share experiential narratives. The IPA researcher is required to be 'present' and empathic. However, counselling students employing IPA need also to be aware of potentially conflicting 'pulls' between ethical application of their roles as therapists and researchers, especially in the exploration of difficult or sensitive materials. Here, Gabriel reflects:

> *I did experience a powerful tension between my research aims and my pull to invoke my practitioner skills and obligations. Mindful of the research topic and potential for role conflict, I aimed to be present in research interviews in a position of 'researcher first'. Despite this aim, some interviews presented particular challenges and I chose to use my therapeutic skills to manage the situation.*
>
> (2009, p149)

Role tension, the management of personal and professional duality and ethical responsibility in research are clear in all forms of research. This is especially the case where methodological and therapeutic approaches fuse in the exploration of potentially rich, invaluable, but sensitive personal and professional materials (Iphofen, 2011).

IPA interviews need to be recorded and transcribed to enable the researcher to extrapolate the riches of each participant's data. On a practical note, it is sensible to test that recording equipment works, and where possible to have a back-up available. Full transcription (which can take around eight hours per hour of interview to complete) is required. Transcription is a time-consuming process, but necessary in order to extract the phenomenological essence of each interview. Modern voice-recognition software can reduce this workload, but given the intensity and the ideographic nature of IPA a sample of between three and six participants is sufficient for smaller-scale studies.

Smith et al. argue:

> Because analysis in IPA aims primarily to interpret the meaning of the **content** of the participant's account, it does not require a particularly detailed transcription of the prosodic aspects of the recordings. That is, it does not require a record of the exact length of pauses, or of all non-verbal utterance as favoured by conversation analysis.
>
> (2009, p74; emphasis in original)

IPA requires researchers to immerse themselves in detailed line-by-line analysis of each transcript in an attempt to extract the phenomenological nuances offered by each participant. The temptation for the novice researcher is to proceed too quickly in generating themes, thereby reducing the potential depth of research inquiry. Only when the process of extracting meaning has been saturated, should the researcher begin to note the emergent themes that are connected within meaning units. Emergent themes are iteratively clustered to generate subordinate themes before the processes are repeated across the research cohort, thereby generating an overarching narrative that is ideographically located in, and representative of, each participant's phenomenological experience. In this way, we can think of IPA as enabling an interpreted 'brick by brick' narrative construction of ideographically located experience (see Figure 8.1 and Table 8.2).

The following is a transcribed extract from a pilot interview undertaken between two students ('T' the interviewer and 'C' the respondent) and analysed within a small, but supportive, seminar group. It is not offered as a 'perfect exemplar' (and indeed demonstrates the importance of completing pilot studies in order to improve different aspects of research), but rather seeks to demonstrate the processes of analytical engagement within IPA.

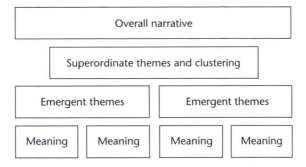

Figure 8.1: 'Brick by brick' narrative construction

IPA values	IPA processes
The uniqueness of the individual's narrative.	Giving time for exploration: semi-structured interviews.
Valuing the way individuals experience their own stories.	Phenomenology – empathy. Building and paying attention to meaning. Retelling participants' stories as they see them themselves.
Co-construction of knowledge.	Reflexivity – how is the researcher and research impacted; how does the researcher impact on the research? Interpretation. Building an overall narrative.

Table 8.2: IPA values and processes

We have deliberately included the extract twice (Tables 8.3 and 8.4), initially without generated themes in order to emphasise the importance of saturating phenomenological meaning, before extracting and connecting emergent themes. In contrast to Smith et al. (2009), we have added an additional column 'Reflexive comments' to the analysis. This column provides researchers with space to note reflexively the influence of their own personal processes on the interpretation and analysis of the data; this is akin to 'memoing' in grounded theory and can be a useful mechanism that augments the validity of the work. This additional column also gives researchers space to record links to the literature that they might become aware of. Reflexive and exploratory commentary should be developed simultaneously, thereby enabling a dynamic and integrated process that pays attention to analysing participants' lived experience and the role of the researcher in its construction.

Original transcripts	Exploratory comments		Reflexive comments
T – 'Could you give me your understanding of what therapist self-disclosure means to you?'			
C – 'It means to me, erm when I have got a teenager and they are experiencing something and I have experienced it, erm I will self-disclose to them that I know how they are feeling cos I have experienced it . . .'	The word 'experience' has been used three times in this response suggesting something personally meaningful to the participant. A depth of feeling. It suggests that self-disclosure offers a meeting or connection point between 'C' and her clients, perhaps as something that 'breaks the ice' or seeks to address or redress difference between client and therapist. Perhaps there is a message: 'We are more alike than you might think.' There is the sense that C wants to be able to interrelate her personal experience with her clients' experiences.		Felt a warmth. Imagine a mother/child relationship – maternal feelings.
T – 'Right, so will use it in that instance?'			
C – 'Yes, in that instance, say that they have got anxiety and they are suffering from panic attacks, because I have anxiety and panic attacks, I have told them about my experience of it and tried to reassure them that they can't kill you and can't harm you.'	C uses a real-life example of shared experience between client and therapist; it seems as if she wants to establish a relationship of reciprocity and mutuality, and one of the ways she feels this can be achieved is by self-disclosure. There is something about C willing to be congruent in the relationship and the way that this is framed is through a willingness to share from her own personal experiences. Reassuring clients seems to be important, or even central,		Appreciation of C's courage and willingness to share. Admiration of vulnerability. To what extent is self-disclosure shared in supervision? To what extent is therapist modality influential? Have I chosen humanistic participants to

Transcript	Exploratory comments	Generated themes
	to C's belief and practice concerning self-disclosure; it feels like almost a kind of mantra. Parallel process. Noticed that participant said 'I have anxiety and panic attacks' – it seems like self-disclosure offers personal reassurance to C as well as her client.	reinforce my beliefs about the positive aspects of self-disclosure? Are there more pluralistic perspectives I could look at? (Cooper and McLeod, 2011)
T – 'That's excellent thank you. Erm, I know it might feel like they are crossing over a little, but I am just wondering about your beliefs around therapist self-disclosure, so you have mentioned there where you would use it, what are your beliefs around disclosure when working with teenagers?'		Recruiting? Collusion? Psychological message: Do you have the same beliefs as me? Blurred the boundaries, dual relationship?
C – 'I think it is more appropriate and accepted by teenagers than it would be by adults, I think it's more erm, I think teenagers like a bit of you in the counselling relationship, it makes it more real for them err . . . I don't think, feel they have the autonomy that an adult has to . . . they have a certain degree of autonomy but I don't	Relational connection points with the young person – mutual acceptance. Wants to be trusted, approachable. There appears to be something suggested here about the nature of the therapeutic bond being premised on openness or transparency even, and that this is expressed through self-disclosure; perhaps too the suggestion that efficacy of the therapeutic bond is reliant on the reciprocation of warmth. Warmth somehow becomes the catalyst for the	Experiencing some of the same feelings, especially when referring to advocacy and the potential 'rescuer' in me. Hearing that a young person needs help would touch something in me about my beliefs about what I'm doing at work in the school. Clash between vocation and the system? Are we (therapists) part of the problem or the cure?

Table 8.3: Sample transcribed excerpt without generated themes (continued overleaf)

Original transcripts	Exploratory comments	Reflexive comments
think they can just work through it by themselves, I think they need a little bit of help.'	therapeutic bond.	Turning my ideas about therapy on their head.
	Differentiating the nature of therapy for teenagers and adults, different needs and expectations perhaps, although this might be a dangerous generalisation.	Foucauldian idea.
	Personal belief – '*I don't think*' – an axiological idea.	This all appears like an additional level of responsibility in therapeutic work with this age group, perhaps leading to a different relational dynamic (parental?).
	Clumping together client group rather than individuals – the word '*they*' is used four times in this response.	Does the perception of the young person of therapy match the therapists' and teachers' perception of therapy?
	'*The autonomy that an adult has*' – comparison between client groups.	
	'*A certain degree of autonomy*' – empowerment – adults hold the power and relinquish or withdraw, somehow the inference is that this client group has some autonomy, but needs help to manage it – in one way it seems as if autonomy is controlled.	
	'I think they need **a little bit** of help' – Help to develop autonomy (rescue?) (I'm doing my little bit) – contribution to support a young person.	
	Assumption that adults have autonomy – '*I don't think, feel they can.*'	
	C expresses something very deep; it seems more than a vocation, almost a passionate sense of calling that is linked with her own identity.	
	There also appears to be a sense of advocacy being presented – siding with the young person in order to advocate on his or her behalf (being a bridge).	

Table 8.3: Continued

Original transcripts	Exploratory comments	Reflexive comments	Emergent themes
T – 'Could you give me your understanding of what therapist self-disclosure means to you?'			
C – 'It means to me, erm when I have got a teenager and they are experiencing something and I have experienced it, erm I will self-disclose to them that I know how they are feeling cos I have experienced it . . .'	The word 'experience' has been used three times in this response suggesting something personally meaningful to the participant. A depth of feeling. It suggests that self-disclosure offers a meeting or connection point between 'C' and her clients, perhaps as something that 'breaks the ice' or seeks to address or redress difference between client and therapist. Perhaps there is a message: 'We are more alike than you might think.' There is the sense that C wants to be able to interrelate her personal experience with her clients' experiences.	Felt a warmth. Imagine a mother/child relationship – maternal feelings	Self-disclosure is personally meaningful. Depth of therapeutic feeling – connection point. Redresses/bridges 'difference' between client and therapist. Mutuality. Makes the relationship more real in working with client group.
T – 'Right, so will use it in that instance?'			

Table 8.4: Sample transcribed excerpt with emergent themes (continued overleaf)

Original transcripts	Exploratory comments	Reflexive comments	Emergent themes
C – 'Yes, in that instance, say that they have got anxiety and they are suffering from panic attacks, because I have anxiety and panic attacks, I have told them about my experience of it and tried to reassure them that they can't kill you and can't harm you.'	C uses a real-life example of shared experience between client and therapist; it seems as if she wants to establish a relationship of reciprocity and mutuality, and one of the ways she feels this can be achieved is by self-disclosure. There is something about C willing to be congruent in the relationship and the way that this is framed is through a willingness to share from her own personal experiences. Reassuring clients seems to be important, or even central, to C's belief and practice concerning self-disclosure; it feels like almost a kind of mantra. Parallel process. Noticed that participant said 'I have anxiety and panic attacks' – it seems like self-disclosure offers personal reassurance to C as well as her client.	Appreciation of C's courage and willingness to share. Admiration of vulnerability. To what extent is self-disclosure shared in supervision? To what extent is therapist modality influential? Have I chosen humanistic participants to reinforce my beliefs about the positive aspects of self-disclosure? Are there more pluralistic perspectives I could look at? (Cooper and McLeod, 2011)	Self-disclosure helps to establish a reciprocal, mutual and trusting relationship between client and counsellor. Self-disclosure as a medium or vehicle of transparency and congruence. Self-disclosure as a mantra of reassurance and connection. (Over?)willingness to share.
T – 'That's excellent thank you. Erm, I know it might feel like they are crossing over a little, but I am just wondering about your		Recruiting? Collusion? Psychological message: Do you have the same beliefs as me?	

beliefs around therapist self-disclosure, so you have mentioned there where you would use it, what are your beliefs around disclosure when working with teenagers?'	Blurred the boundaries, dual relationship?	Self-disclosure fosters mutuality and trust between therapist and young people. Self-disclosure promotes 'realness' in the relationship. Counselling young people is different from counselling adults; they have different needs, processes and expectations. Young people experience different levels of autonomy from adults in different domains, including therapy; therapist disclosure redresses imbalances and fosters the management of adolescent autonomy. Deep sense of vocation to counsel young people: links to self-disclosure as a mantra.
C – 'I think it is more appropriate and accepted by teenagers than it would be by adults, I think it's more erm, I think teenagers like a bit of you in the counselling relationship, it makes it more real for them err . . . I don't think, feel they have the autonomy that an adult has to . . . they have a certain degree of autonomy but I don't think they can just work through it by themselves, I think they need a little bit of help.'	Relational connection points with the young person – mutual acceptance. Wants to be trusted, approachable. There appears to be something suggested here about the nature of the therapeutic bond being premised on openness or transparency even, and that this is expressed through self-disclosure; perhaps too the suggestion that efficacy of the therapeutic bond is reliant on the reciprocation of warmth. Warmth somehow becomes the catalyst for the therapeutic bond. Differentiating the nature of therapy for teenagers and adults, different needs and expectations perhaps; however; this might be a dangerous generalisation. Personal belief – 'I don't think' – an axiological idea.	Experiencing some of the same feelings, especially when referring to advocacy and the potential 'rescuer' in me. Hearing that a young person needs help would touch something in me about my beliefs about what I'm doing at work in the school. Clash between vocation and the system? Are we (therapists) part of the problem or the cure? Turning my ideas about therapy on their head. Foucauldian idea. This all appears like an additional level of responsibility in therapeutic work with this

Table 8.4: Continued

Original transcripts	Exploratory comments	Reflexive comments	Emergent themes
	Clumping together client group rather than individuals – the word *'they'* is used four times in this response.	age group, perhaps leading to a different relational dynamic (parental?).	
	'The autonomy that an adult has' – comparison between client groups.	Does the perception of the young person of therapy match the therapists' and teachers' perception of therapy?	
	'A certain degree of autonomy' – empowerment – adults hold the power and relinquish or withdraw, somehow the inference is that this client group has some autonomy, but needs help to manage it – in one way it seems as if autonomy is controlled.		
	'I think they need **a little bit** of help' – Help to develop autonomy (rescue?) (I'm doing my little bit) – contribution to support a young person.		
	Assumption that adults have autonomy – *'I don't think, feel they can'*		
	C expresses something very deep; it seems more than a vocation, almost a passionate sense of calling that is linked with her own identity.		
	There also appears to be a sense of advocacy being presented – siding with the young person in order to advocate on his or her behalf (being a bridge).		

Table 8.4: Continued

The first analytical stage (as with all forms of qualitative research) requires researchers to immerse themselves in the data by reading and rereading the transcript. They will then begin to systematically generate initial notes by interrogating the data line by line. Some passages within the interview might contain richer data, and legitimately require greater analysis and commentary. Although not prescribed, this stage of phenomenological analysis may generate descriptive commentary that elucidates the context and experience of participants' lifeworlds, linguistic commentary that explores how language is constructed and used to convey phenomenological meaning within given ideographic contexts, and conceptual commentary that might be linked to subject literature or theoretical ideas, and which is often framed interrogatively (ibid.).

This phase of the analysis may need to be repeated several times in order to ensure iterative engagement and phenomenological saturation. When satisfied that the data has been saturated, the researcher is able to begin searching for emergent themes. This we might think of as a process of phenomenological reduction in which the researcher condenses the rich language of description generated in exploratory and reflexive commentary to a more essentialist form, yet which remains true to the data.

The researcher's role now becomes more concerned with looking for patterns and interconnections in the data. The researcher needs to simultaneously extract potential thematic connections in specific passages of the data, while being able to connect these emergent themes with what has been previously uncovered. In this sense, this phase of analysis is grounded more fully in the *interpretative* element of IPA, and can be seen as the bridge between the phenomenological reporting of the first stage of analysis and conceptual generation that characterises the latter stages.

The next stage of analysis requires the researcher to generate connections between emergent themes. This process of 'jigsawing' the data enables the researcher to connect and construct constituent elements of the data in a way that makes sense. The researcher seeks to cluster emergent themes and to engage in a process of abstract conceptualisation.

Practically, this can be achieved by recording emergent themes on movable sticky notes, which can be iteratively grouped in order to generate superordinate themes that thematically represent the overarching essence of the data in a few sentences. Such patternation can also highlight the importance of a theme based on the emphasis it is given or the frequency with which it occurs. The researcher repeats the process across the cohort, seeking as far as possible to bracket off ideas that emerge in preceding cases that might taint the analysis of subsequent transcripts. Upon completion, the researcher seeks to make interconnections between superordinate themes across the entire cohort with the purpose of generating master themes that summatively represent the narrated experience of each participant and from which tentative, ideographically located conceptualisations can be offered for consideration and further research. In writing up the research, direct quotations from transcripts should be used to illustrate and validate the themes and concepts being advanced.

From the themes that have emerged from the excerpted transcript in Table 8.4, two superordinate themes (which may have become subsumed into other themes had the *entire* interview been analysed) can be generated, and taken forward for master theme subsumption.

The participant believes and experiences the following.

1. Young people are a discrete client group with particular needs, processes and expectations. They experience diverse levels of autonomy, and power differentials in relation to adults in a range of domains including therapy, which therapist self-disclosure seeks to mitigate.
2. Self-disclosure provides a connection point between the therapist and adolescent clients, enabling the establishment of a reciprocal, mutually founded relationship that fosters genuineness and trust.

While those who avow IPA consider it a framework founded in particular axiological and ontological positions rather than a formulaic approach to research requiring rigid adherence, many novice researchers prefer for surety's sake to follow IPA's framework systematically.

ACTIVITY 8.2

Earlier in this chapter we advised that research should be 'piloted' in order that biases might be identified and interview schedules refined.

- Look at the excerpted transcript (Table 8.4); how might you develop the questions asked?

Internal validity of qualitative research is concerned with generating arguments that are sufficiently supported and sustained by the data (see Chapter 9). While readers have not engaged in the '3D' collection and analysis of the above data, afforded through live interaction between participants, you should be able to offer evaluation of the validity of the superordinate themes listed above.

- Discuss with others the degree to which the data is able to sustain the arguments generated in the themes. What might be improved?

THE BASIS OF THE QUANTITATIVE APPROACH

As we know, at its simplest, research is about answering questions (Reeves, 2013). It is about learning something new; about acquiring new knowledge. However, the sorts of knowledge that are being acquired will very much depend on the sorts of questions being asked and the ways in which the answers are produced (Claringbull, 2010). In other words, the types of knowledge any given research project generates depends on the types of enquiries that are made and how the results are presented and explained (see Cohen et al., 2011).

Many modern researchers argue that knowledge arises from one of two main philosophical traditions (Sanders and Wilkins, 2010, p5). They claim that it is either subjective (derived from situationally influenced interpretations of events) or objective (derived from impartial observations of reality). Consider the following two examples.

Example 1: We might want to know if clients value their counsellors. In such a case, subjective answers might be the more informative and so we ask a representative group of clients to tell us about their therapists. Then we collate their stories and interpret them qualitatively. We might use discourse analysis, IPA or any other suitable qualitative approach. Certainly no numbers are involved.

Example 2: We need to reassure some counselling service funders that their money is being well spent. In this case, objective (quantitative) answers are essential and so we measure the psychological 'temperatures' of a sample client group on a 'before-and-after therapy' basis in order to evaluate their progress. Numbers are very much involved.

So, which style of investigation is 'best', qualitative or quantitative? Clearly this dichotomy generates debate and so sets up tensions between knowledge gatherers (Muran et al., 2010, p4). Therefore, a key question that all researchers must ask themselves is: 'What sort of knowledge (subjective or objective) are we gathering'? In this part of Chapter 8 we shall be focusing on objective knowledge. This is the sort of learning that is derived from quantitative (numbers-based) enquiries.

However, gathering the numbers is only the beginning. Next comes finding ways of drawing conclusions from them. For example, suppose that a quantitative investigation into our clients' well-being tells us that clients who scored an average of 40 per cent on a happiness scale before counselling scored an average of 62 per cent afterwards. These figures apparently suggest that therapy is helpful, but is this really true? Can we rely on these findings?

Are the differences between the 'before' and 'after' scores large enough to be really convincing? Perhaps these differences have only come about by chance and by themselves mean nothing. What if the post-therapy average was only 43 per cent? Would that still mean that counselling is a 'good thing'?

ACTIVITY 8.3

Assume that you carried out five different 'happiness' surveys for the clients of five different counselling agencies and got the following results.

Happiness	Agency 1	Agency 2	Agency 3	Agency 4	Agency 5
Before therapy %	58	32	43	53	61
After therapy %	60	65	61	62	15

You have £10,000 to purchase counselling services in your area. There are no rules about who gets what, but you must get maximum value for money. You also happen to know that if any agency gets less than £3,000 it will have to close.

- Decide how to share out the money. Should some agencies get more than others? Should any get nothing? Justify your decisions.

CONTROLLING THE RESEARCH

Another question that counselling and psychotherapy researchers must always ask themselves is – 'how can we be sure that the changes observed in clients are solely due to their treatments'? Researchers need to be reasonably confident that other factors, perhaps events occurring outside the therapy room, were not the real causes of the changes. The usual way around this difficulty is to divide the clients into two groups. One group (the Treated Group) gets therapy and the other group (the Control Group) does not. If the treated clients do appreciably better than the controls, we might be able to argue that therapy is *probably* better than no therapy. 'Probably' has been highlighted because, as we shall see, an understanding of *probability* is essential for anyone who wants to critique quantitative research.

For example, let us suppose that we want to know if behavioural therapy is a useful treatment for depression. We select a group of depressed patients from an NHS waiting list and assess all of them using Beck's Depression Inventory (BDI). Each patient is then randomly allocated to either a Treated List or a Control List. All the patients on the Treated List are given six behavioural therapy sessions. Those on the Control List remain untreated. In essence we are carrying out a randomised controlled trial (RCT – see Chapter 5). Six months later all these patients, treated and untreated alike, are reassessed. Just to make sure that we have tested a reasonably representative sample of patients we repeat this investigation in two other NHS districts. The results are as follows.

District 1	Before	After	District 2	Before	After	District 3	Before	After
Treated (Average BDI)	28	9	Treated (Average BDI)	26	7	Treated (Average BDI)	28	13
Untreated (Average BDI)	27	11	Untreated (Average BDI)	27	28	Untreated (Average BDI)	27	18

1. In District 1 most of the patients got better, treated or not – behavioural therapy does not appear to have had any effect.
2. In District 2 the treated patients mostly improved and the untreated patients did not – behavioural therapy appears to be effective.
3. In District 3 both groups improved to a certain extent – these results appear to be somewhat inconclusive.

Note: Suppose that the particular set of results found in District 2 had also been found in the other two districts and perhaps elsewhere in the NHS too. Finding such an extensive set of positive outcomes would be likely to encourage the uptake of behavioural therapy as a treatment of choice for depression. Any such resulting research-based developments in patient management would, in effect, be examples of evidence-based practice in action (see Chapter 3).

However, in fact the results, as set out above, are actually quite confusing. Is behavioural therapy helpful or not? One way of resolving this puzzle might be to combine the results from the three studies and see what the numbers tell us, if taken as a whole. Are they going in any particular direction? Perhaps we could also analyse our findings in conjunction with findings from other similar research projects (a 'meta-study'). Doing that might help us to reliably identify a possible general trend. 'Reliability' is the key word here.

There are no certainties in counselling and psychotherapy research. Absolute proof is impossible (Coolican, 2013), replicating results is extremely difficult (Pashler and Wagenmakers, 2012) and generalising research findings into predicable(*ish*) therapeutic 'laws' is, at best, contentious (Ritchie and Lewis, 2003). However, we can ask ourselves 'what is the *probability* that what we have found is true? How far can we trust our findings?

PROBABILITY

The good news is that we can actually calculate a trustworthiness level or a 'truth rating' (probability) for any of our quantitative research findings. This rating ranges from 'Probably Untrue' to 'Probably True'. If we know the truth ratings for a particular set of enquiries, we can better decide how much we can rely on them. For instance, suppose that three positive studies of treatments X, Y and Z have trustworthiness levels of 60, 90 and 95 per cent respectively. If we know what these truth ratings are telling us, we have a basis for deciding which treatments to adopt and which to reject.

Understanding the concept of probability is the key to appreciating quantitative research. What are the chances (the probability) that the effects that we are observing are due to our therapeutic inputs and not simply random events that would have happened anyway? Does our evidence really suggest that treatment Type Y is likely to be effective in certain cases? What are the chances that we are right?

TAKING A CHANCE

If you toss a coin, then it is 50–50 which side up it lands. Do this a lot of times and the overall results are likely to show more or less equal numbers of heads and tails appearing. So, let us pretend that you are betting against someone else in a game based on coin tossing. That person scores two heads in a row; OK, that is the luck of the game. Three heads? – OK. Four heads? – Hmm! Fifty heads? – Cheat!! Of course it is possible, in theory at least, that a phenomenally lucky player could score fifty heads in a row. Possible yes, but you are unlikely to believe that such a game is really being played honestly. The reason that you suspect cheating is that your opponent's results are obviously very different from those that would be likely if the heads/tails outcomes were occurring purely randomly. The core question is this. If two heads in a row is probably fair and if fifty heads in a row is probably cheating, where is the fair/unfair boundary point?

There is another very important question that researchers must always ask themselves. It lies at the very heart of counselling and psychotherapy research and it is this. Are the observed outcomes of a series of tests really caused by the researchers' experimental manipulations or are they just random happenstance? Remember, a random result is one where outcome A is as likely as outcome B.

PLAYING THE ODDS

In life generally we play the odds and we make decisions about which odds are acceptable. Sometimes we are happy to accept poor odds. For example, it is millions to one against winning the Lottery but we still might cheerfully risk a £1. Sometimes we are not so carefree. For instance, we would not go up in an aircraft if we thought there was a 5 per cent chance that it might crash. That would not be an acceptable level of risk. It is a well-established truism that there are no certainties in life or indeed in science. Even the sun might fail to rise one day! Risk can never be eliminated; it can only be kept within bounds. That is what we try to do when we plan our counselling and psychotherapy research projects. We want to reduce the risk of being wrong.

The distinguished philosopher, Karl Popper, illustrated our inability to achieve 100 per cent scientific certainty with his 'white swan' paradigm (Popper, 1972). It goes like this. Assume that our research findings so far have led us to hypothesise that all swans are white. However, we can never conclusively prove that theory because there is always a possibility that the next swan we see will be black. In other words, science can only absolutely prove a negative – 'having seen just one black swan, I am now 100 per cent certain that they are not all white'. Therefore, we can only remain reasonably confident that all swans are white until we see a black one. The question is: 'just how confident'?

As Popper clearly shows us, research can never prove that something is true. All it can do is give us a good reason to reject the possibility (for now at least) that something is untrue. If we can reject the negative then, by default, we can *infer* the positive. If we know with what degree of certainty we can reject the negative we also know just how likely it is that the positive is the true result and not merely the result of random chance. In other words, in all counselling and psychotherapy research, both qualitative and quantitative alike, we play the odds. The difference between these two methodologies is that in the case of quantitative research we can work out just what odds actually are.

An example

Let us suppose that we want to further explore Hans Eysenck's great question 'does psychotherapy work?' (Claringbull, 2010, p14; Lambert, 2013, p4). We decide that a randomised controlled trial (RCT) will best suit our purposes. We therefore randomly assign some psychologically distressed people into two groups, treat one group and ignore the other group. The extra input that the treatment group gets is called the *variable*. You will find the RCT process explained in more detail in Chapter 5.

Our experimental assumption is that any improvements in the untreated group occur at random. We want to know if introducing a variable (the treatment) causes any non-random outcomes; does the treatment work? Having employed one of the standard 'before-and-after' outcome measures, we get the following results.

Distress level	Before	After
Treated	10	5
Untreated	6	6

Our enquiries can only have one of two possible results.

1. The treatment did not have an effect – *the null hypothesis*.
2. The treatment did have an effect – *the alternative hypothesis*.

Remember, we cannot prove that the treatment works. All we can do is to find good grounds for suggesting that our clients got better by design and not by chance. We do this by assessing just how safely we can reject the null hypothesis. What are the chances that, by so doing, we would be making a mistake? The more certain we are that we can safely reject the null hypothesis, the more certain we can be about inferring that treatment works.

Many statisticians would argue that the *chi square test* is useful for analysing the sorts of results listed above. If you want to know more about this particular test, you might find that Miles and Banyard (2007, pp169–93) is a good place to start. We shall not be offering you a maths lesson here.

As it happens, for this particular set of results, calculations based on the chi square test tell us that the odds are 99–1 that the null hypothesis is untrue. We can fairly safely reject it. This allows us to infer that the alternative hypothesis is viable. Therefore, we can say that we have good evidence to suggest that, in this case at least, psychotherapy works.

Note: we have NOT proved that psychotherapy works nor have we proved that it works 99 per cent of the time. We have definitely not shown that psychotherapy is the best treatment for psychological distress. All we have done is to suggest that it is quite reasonable to surmise that, in some cases, psychotherapy might benefit our clients.

THE MATHEMATICAL BIT

In mathematical terms the level of probability we determine is the level of *statistical significance* that we can give to our findings. Probability, '*p*', is assessed on a scale from 0 to 1 where 1 means that it would be totally wrong to reject the null hypothesis and 0 means that it would be totally safe to do so. In the psychological sciences, we have long assumed that, in order to safely reject the null hypothesis, we need *p* to be 0.05 or lower (Fisher, 1925; Yates, 2004, p96 and many others). This means that the chances of making the wrong decision are 1 in 20 (5%) or less. However, it should also be noted that there is ongoing debate about whether or not $p = 0.05$ is the correct cut-off point – see Activity 8.4.

Do not worry about the maths. Just concern yourself with the under-lying principles. You can learn the 'numbers bit' another time. What you do need to know is just what the numbers mean when you encounter them. The problem is that numbers look authoritative. However, that does not mean that we always have to trust them. We need to be able to unpick them.

Remember . . .

1. All the numbers in the world are useless if the research was carried out poorly – garbage in really does equal garbage out.
2. Another big problem is that of *generalisation*. For example, does research carried out on a sample of fifty widows all aged over 70 really tell us anything about how to help a group of depressed, pregnant teenagers?
3. What is the level of *prior probability*? How inevitable were the research outcomes? How much do we trust the researchers to be really open-minded? For example, a new study by Greenpeace that tells us that we should decrease our use of fossil fuels would not be much of an eye opener. However, if the Soil Association was to tell us that they could no longer find any benefits from eating organic food, we would certainly want to take note.

LEARNING ABOUT STATISTICS

First the good news – we will not be learning how to carry out statistical analysis here. However, if you want to go any further down that road, and we would very much like to encourage you to do so, why not have a look at one of the books listed in the suggested further reading list opposite.

Second, the even better news – you do not have to become a mathematical genius in order to carry out quantitative research. There is a very clever computer program called SPSS (originally called the Statistical Package for the Social Sciences) that does it all for you. This very useful piece of software takes all the hard work out of statistics. It lets you easily use the power of numbers to give your investigations added strength.

The reality is that modern counselling and psychotherapy researchers no longer have to choose between qualitative and quantitative methodologies. They refuse to weaken their investigations by restricting themselves to any particular approach. Modern researchers use any methodology, in any combination, whenever they need to. In today's therapeutic world, for practitioners and researchers alike, the watchword is 'pluralism'. Whatever works, works!

ACTIVITY 8.4

Not everybody agrees that p should be set at 0.05 for psychological and social science research (see the review in Miles and Banyard, 2007, pp307–19). After all, as we know, the traditional sciences demand very much smaller values for p.

- Should counselling and psychotherapy researchers be more demanding or less so? Make a list of p values that you would find acceptable.
- Would you accept different p levels in different circumstances? A success rate of, say, 60 per cent would not be acceptable in engineering, but it might be good enough in psychotherapy. What do you think?

CHAPTER SUMMARY

In this chapter, we have sought to offer readers insight into the application of two methodologies and further discussed the values and ideas that underpin them, thereby enabling practitioner-researchers to further consider the value of different types of knowledge for different purposes. In doing so, we hope to have demystified aspects of the research process and to have made the application of ideas more accessible.

SUGGESTED FURTHER READING

Miles, J and Banyard, P (2007) *Understanding and Using Statistics in Psychology: A practical introduction.* London: Sage.

This is a very easy read written in a light-hearted, user-friendly style. If your mathematical skills are at about GCSE grade C, you will have no difficulty whatsoever getting on with this book.

Rumsey, D (2010) *Statistics Essentials for Dummies.* Hoboken, NJ: Wiley.

Aspiring statisticians, whether absolute beginners or above, will all find something in this book. Even counsellors and psychotherapists will find it easy to read.

Rumsey, D (2011) *Statistics for Dummies*, 2nd edition. Hoboken, NJ: Wiley.

Does exactly what it says on the tin. This is a book for everyone, mathematically literate or not.

CHAPTER 9

How was it for you?

Graham Bright

CORE KNOWLEDGE

By the end of this chapter, you will be able to:

- analyse and apply evaluatory perspectives;
- evaluate the validity of your research;
- appraise the impact of your work.

Congratulations! It is likely that you will be reading this chapter for two reasons, at critical and exciting points in the research process. First, you may be referring to this chapter to consider ways in which you can *ensure* the validity of the work as a *process*. Second, you may be revisiting this chapter as you near the completion and submission of your work to *evaluate* the validity of your research as a *product*, and to consider reflexively the impact that this learning journey has had on you and on others around you.

Validity is about ethics. It is principally concerned with telling the truth and ensuring that the research processes employed in a study are suitably robust and fit for their intended purpose. Validity is therefore focused on the question: 'Do researchers see what they think they see?' Clearly, validity matters in order that researchers can properly and truthfully represent data in a way that upholds personal and professional integrity and that honours the trust placed in researchers by participants. Evaluating the validity of research therefore requires the researcher to hold parallel positions: one that recognises the researcher's own place in the work with all the potentially deep emotional and intellectual learning that this catalyses, while simultaneously being able to assume the role of the more objective observer who critically seeks to ensure that the work is representative of the data generated and the 'truths' being told.

In commencing this chapter, therefore, it is important that we consider what truth means. From a positivist worldview, the notion of truth is perhaps more easily encapsulated and defined as being absolutist – a paradigm that is in some way 'provable', testable and generalisable, where facts are objectively pinpointed via science-based inquiry. Yet, as we have been examining more fully in this text, truth in the context of the socially constructed, postmodern and therapeutic worlds is often a more subjective affair that is rooted in multifaceted realities navigated through words, stories, pictures and meanings.

Truth is formed in streams of consciousness. Despite apparent nebulousness, there remains a crucial ethical and moral obligation (irrespective of particular epistemological stances) on researchers to represent their research findings in a truthful fashion and to demonstrate the suitability and rigorous application of chosen methodologies in such a way that legitimates them. Truth in this sense is concerned with the authenticity, transparency and reliability of the research and the integrity of the researcher. The ethical weight of truth-telling in research can be seen if we refer to professional ethical frameworks (e.g. BACP, 2010), which describe the integral nature of fidelity, non-maleficence, beneficence and justice as applied to professional practice and by implication to research. As Wilkins notes, *it is the plausibility and the trustworthiness of the researcher which speaks to the validity of the findings* (2010, p220). The onus of ethical responsibility for telling the truth in research is therefore clearly embodied in, and inextricably linked to, the integrity of the researcher him- or herself. Objectivity within research that concerns the subjective is by nature a direction of travel rather than a specifically designated arrival point. Yet it remains important in qualitative research to travel that road while capturing the sounds, smells, emotions, meanings and colours of particular human experiences in order to represent faithfully these truths in research outputs. Reflexivity is crucial here in order that the researcher can continually and symbiotically examine and bring to awareness the complex interrelationships between the research, the researched and the researcher's own multifaceted configurations of self (Mearns and Thorne, 2007).

Truth, we might argue, is an intellectually and philosophically challenging notion. Silverman (2009) advises that, instead of metaphysically pursuing truth as a vague concept, we should be more concerned with evaluating the credibility of research work. The concept of truth has been further clouded in an era that distrusts or even lacks the grand narratives of the past. Muncey, in this instance, argues the importance of understanding and validating individual micro-narratives, and articulates this beautifully when she writes *truth and story are honourable companions* (2011, p107). We could argue that micro-biographies that are reflective of the postmodern project might be bricolaged through research in order to create a sense of inter-linking ideographies that form and validate a meso-narrative understanding of the world in particular (therapeutic) contexts. In this vein, McLeod (2011b) encourages researchers to ensure that sufficient information about participants is included in the work in order that readers get a fuller sense of, and can make better informed judgements about, research.

Validity in its different forms therefore requires researchers to ensure that evidence 'stacks up' coherently and corroboratively in enabling the resonant construction of robust arguments. In this sense, we might use the analogy of a criminal investigation where different forms of evidence (including storied accounts) from a range of sources are collected, cross-examined and corroborated in order to reach well-informed conclusions that can stand up to scrutinous interrogation (Eisner, 1991, in Creswell, 2007). Parker (2005) argues that the validity of research is concerned with its stability. Whereas positivist forms of controlled research have greater capacity to ensure stability through clinical trialling and the control of variables that aid the construction of important and compelling arguments in different academic and applied domains, including counselling and psychotherapy, via statistical outcomes from large cohorts, there remains the question of how to enable the construction of robust and validatable arguments gathered through the range of qualitative methodologies. Here we need a paradigm shift in order to ensure that we consider issues of validity, reliability and objectivity in qualitative terms, rather than seeking to compare and apply positivist values to interpretivist practices. We require, as the adage goes, to 'compare oranges with oranges, not oranges with apples'.

Citing the work of Lincoln and Guba (1985), Finlay and Evans (2009), as summarised in Table 9.1, argue for qualitative equivalences to traditional validity indicators that are grounded in, but not transferable from, positivism.

Here, Spinelli posits that:

> . . . legitimate Human Science enquiry involves alternative notions to those of Natural Science enquiry. These include terms like trustworthiness, credibility, dependability, and confirmability and are intended to re-contextualise the Natural Science notion of validity within a Human Science arena.
>
> (2010, p130)

The criteria therefore for validity in qualitative work, as framed by its reliability and capacity for objectivity, are different from those in quantitative research for which criteria are more prescriptively detailed. Creswell argues that there are *polyvocal discourses* (2007, p201) evident between qualitative researchers, but that assessment of research should be premised on establishing the 'credibility' and 'authenticity' of research. For Finlay and Evans validity is grounded in evidencing that the research *has been systematically and conscientiously conducted* (2009, p59). In qualitative work, we must therefore consider the role of the researcher's influence on

Type of positivistic measure	Definition	A qualitative 'equivalent'
Internal validity	The capacity and sustainability of the data to support the arguments being made.	Credibility – ways in which the research findings are plausible and make sense.
External validity/ generalisability	The degree to which research findings can be generalised to wider populations based on a range of factors including spatial, temporal and institutional dimensions.	Transferability, supplying sufficient information in order that readers can make informed decisions about whether findings can be transferred to related contexts, thereby indicating relevance that augments the current body of knowledge.
Reliability and objectivity	Reliability is about the capacity of research to be replicated over time in similar contexts with similar cohorts and producing similar results. Positivist objectivity seeks to eliminate biases from research processes in order that generated data can be viewed as 'uncontaminated'.	Dependability and confirmability are concerned with ensuring that the researcher has enabled the generation and interrogation of the data robustly, and has produced an 'audit trail', including detailed engagement with ethical protocols that demonstrate transparency and rigour.

Table 9.1: Qualitative equivalences to traditional validity indicators
(after Lincoln and Guba, 1985; Finlay and Evans, 2009)

the research. For the qualitative researcher in whom kernels of research are heuristically catalysed, the research process interweaves personal micro-narratives with the emergent meso-narrative in which he or she is an active maieutic participant. The qualitative researcher is not the dispassionate archetypical white-coated researcher (Wilkins, 2010; Bager-Charleson, 2012); his or her engagement is rather different. Clearly, therefore, it is important not only to evaluate reflectively the truthfulness of research as a product by considering its ongoing validity and reliability, but to plan and consider truthfulness as a process. Here, the interrogation of self and self with others of research ideas, processes and findings, together with the transparency of the researcher's own clearly expressed subjective axiological and ontological positioning, are essential to the development of reflexive capacities that ensure the robustness and value of the work (Etherington, 2004; May and Perry, 2011). Establishing a rigorous relationship between the research aims, objectives, questions and outcomes (see Bright and Harrison, Chapter 4, this volume) (while recognising that research can enable unanticipated discoveries – which should not, however, become unhelpful divergences to the research in hand), together with a rationalised and transparently executed methodology, is central to research validity. While positivist research may be able to make grander claims of generalisability, qualitative researchers should, given the ideographic and temporal nature of their work, be more cautious about such assertions. As McLeod (2007a) points out, the dynamic interplay between particular research participants, a particular researcher, in a particular time and place is likely to give rise to different results when carried out in different, albeit similar, circumstances, and broader, interrelated research around the same topic may need to be generated in order to validate more generalised claims. This does not, however, detract from the power or validity of narrative forms of socially constructed knowledge; nevertheless, qualitative researchers are called not only to recognise the validity of ideographic experience, but also to be wise about the claims they make. Yardley argues that qualitative researchers should *aspire to what can be called 'theoretical', 'vertical', or 'logical' rather than statistical generalisations* (2009, p238), in order that implied or potential transferability of research can be evaluated and 'trialled' in cognate contexts.

In these ways, as Parker notes:

> *Qualitative researchers [are able to] work with subjectivity rather than against it . . . good qualitative research often focuses on change and traces a process, rather than treating patterns of human behaviour or thinking as things that are fixed.*
>
> (2005, pp136–7)

Parker further examines challenges of intersubjectivity between researcher and participants. He argues the inevitability of (at least partially) describing and analysing data from the perspective of the researcher; and, while we cannot and should not underestimate the power of the researcher's role in qualitative research, we can seek to ensure the greater validity of the work through a range of processes.

Here again reflexivity is central. For Etherington, validity:

> *rests on questions about: whether researcher reflexivity has provided enough information about the social, cultural, historical, racial, sexual context in which all the stories are located; if multiple voices give broad enough perspectives to take in different views; if the style of representation offers*

enough openings to creative expression; and finally, if the work contributes to our understanding and new learning about the subject of inquiry.

(2004, p82)

Finlay and Evans make the plea that quality in relationally grounded qualitative research should be viewed in terms of *clarity and accessibility* (2009, p59); research should be challenging, but not impregnable, and should deepen therapeutic praxis. As a marker of validity, qualitative research should generate resonance through the dripping detail of rich description, which touches both researcher and reader emotionally and spiritually, leaving its own impactive marks (ibid.). Resonance in this sense relates to transformational, affective and catalytic validity through which research illuminates processes of change and catalyses transformation.

Case study 9.1

In a recent piece of research (Bright, 2011), I wanted to explore with pupil-clients the influence school counselling had on the development of personal resilience in the face of a range of challenging personal, social and educational circum-stances. I was committed to ensuring the work represented participants' experiences, and sought (especially during the pilot phase of the research) to ask participants their views on the research in order that I could reflect on and improve the research sub-questions for the main study.

After the first pilot interview, I somewhat nervously asked my participant, 16-year-old 'James', what he thought and felt about the interview we had just conducted. He responded: 'It's been really good; it has made me think about things. It's helped me think about how things used to be and how far I have come. It's made me realise how much counselling has actually helped . . . and in some ways because I've not been to counselling for a few months now, it has helped me realise how strong I have actually become. It has almost been as good as the counselling itself.'

Affective catalytic validity is clear. The research process gave James the opportunity to reflect on the processes and outcomes of therapy in a way that helped him to understand and consolidate therapeutic gains, and enabled me to further consider aspects of the research process.

Catalytic validity has the power to enact change. Forms of action research that are completed, for example, in the context of counselling organisations, together with research that has an explicitly emancipatory stance, are prime examples that often resonate in bringing about transformation in thinking and practice within therapeutic contexts. Greater validity can be achieved where research is collaborative – where it is carried out with, rather than on, participants. Collaborative and emancipatory forms of research have the power to appropriately engage participants in the chronological expanse of research processes from formulation to data gathering and analyses checking (Reason and Heron, 2003). Asking participants to comment on the accuracy of data transcription and analysis can therefore be a helpful way of augmenting the validity of the work.

ACTIVITY 9.1

Examine three pieces of published counselling research that may or may not be related to your own particular research interests. Consider the following questions.

- What is the research about?
- Has the research been sufficiently contextualised within appropriate domains?
- How has the research been conducted? Is there sufficient information with which to judge the suitability, robustness and ethical application of the research processes employed?
- What claims does the research make?
- How would you evaluate the internal validity or credibility of the work? Do the data sufficiently support the claims or arguments being made?
- How have the research outcomes been corroborated?

Discuss your findings with others in your group.

- What can be learned for your own research?
- What objections might readers raise about the validity of your research?
- How do you plan to enhance the validity of your work?

Eisner argues that: *We seek a confluence of evidence that breeds credibility, that allows us to feel confident about our observations, interpretations and conclusions* (1991, p110, cited in Creswell, 2007, p204). Demonstrating validity therefore requires the construction of various forms of corroborative 'proofs'. A primary way in which such evidence can be constructed is by *triangulation*, which in its original context *refers to the practice of calculating location from three different reference points* (Yardley, 2009, p239). In research terms triangulation is concerned with providing a framework for constructing arguments that utilise data from diverse yet convergent sources to enable a sense of corroborative orientation and congruence in the data. Validative triangulation can be generated in different ways by enabling mutual and interweaving connections between research touchstones.

First, triangulated perspectives can be produced through *methodological pluralism* (McLeod, 2007a, p181), which generates data from the same cohort, or even the same research participant, by using different research methodologies or data collection methods. In this instance, participants may contribute, for example, to a semi-structured interview utilising Interpretative Phenomenological Analysis, and answer some Likert scaling questions or respond to a questionnaire. Similarly, if empirical research is being conducted in a number of stages over time, it may be justifiable to utilise different qualitative and/or quantitative methodologies with different sub-cohorts in producing and triangulating data.

For example, participants may agree to take part in a focus group, which enables formative phenomenological exploration and the refinement of research questions, while participating later in an episodic narrative inquiry, which further contextualises the focus group research and the research question within participant lifecourses. Second, researchers may work collaboratively with others in gathering and analysing data. This form of joint endeavour gives rise to investigator or researcher triangulation in which perspectives are synergised and personal biases counterbalanced. Third, we can consider theoretical triangulation in which the researcher is able to explore through primary and secondary data sources (including the literature review) different theoretical perspectives on given phenomena in arriving at well-considered, rather than narrow and predetermined, arguments. Finally, as Flick argues, researchers can engage in *data triangulation* (2009, p444), which draws empirically on the narratives, experiences and responses of different research participants within a defined sample in different spaces at different times. Here, triangulating data by comparison of experiences across a data cohort is integral. In this way, for example, a researcher may wish to interview counsellors from a range of theoretical orientations who work in or across local, regional or national organisational contexts over a six-month period about a given phenomenon. As Dallos and Vetere note, triangulation *enhance[s] our understanding whilst at the same time [providing] a basis for cross-checking and cross-referencing our findings* (2005, p205), while, for McLeod, *The aim of triangulation is to find agreement about the core meanings or themes . . . The act of interpretation involves locating the meaning of an experience or event within the context of a larger set of meanings* (2007a, p86–7).

In concluding this section, therefore, we can summarise that a number of important, practical checkpoints are key in seeking to ensure the validity of research.

(Qualitative) researchers should (after McLeod, 2007a, p94–6):

- make research processes transparent by including 'procedural detail';
- ensure that the study is sufficiently and sensitively contextualised *in its historical, social and cultural location* (McLeod, 2007a, p94);
- ensure clear linkages between data and emergent theoretical positions;

- rationalise and justify research outcomes that clearly explain data interpretations over other potential discourses;
- develop rich description;
- triangulate data to corroborate their integrity;
- ask participants to reflect on interview experiences to elucidate potential affective and catalytic validities;
- ensure clarity of process in order that it might be replicated by others, while recognising the uniqueness of ideography.

ACTIVITY 9.2

- Discuss with others how you have triangulated, or plan to triangulate, your data. Consider engaging in a peer-review process that explicitly examines ways in which research is triangulated and validated.

This chapter is principally concerned with evaluation, which we can define as *assessing and judging the value of a piece of work, an organisation or a service* (Evaluation Trust, 2012). To this point we have considered ways in which research processes and products might be evaluated and their quality enhanced by enabling readers to reflect on how they can generate ethical, truthful and robust work. It is imperative, however, not only to consider learning about the topic that has been investigated, but also to reflect on the researcher's own personal and affective learning. For counsellors, irrespective of modality, personal learning within the context of life and professional development is fundamental (Bager-Charleson, 2012; Johns, 2012). Hall (2012) describes the power of the written word as a means of fostering counsellors' personal development; it may be that you engaged with the suggestion offered in Chapter 1 to keep a research diary as an aid to encapsulating learning – it may equally be that this was not for you. Irrespective of this, it is likely that you have participated in a journey that has enabled some form of professional and personal discovery. In reaching the end of this particular research expedition, it is important to capture and process that learning. Perhaps there are things to reflect on personally, or with others who have been fellow travellers.

Counselling is a heuristic activity, grounded in embracing processes of discovery for both client and counsellor. Questions that we ask come from somewhere: interconnected experiences, memories (both known and denied) and human inquisitiveness weave together to help us wonder. Questions about counselling are no different; they arise from interactions with clients, supervisors, trainers and fellow therapists in a way that blends with our own personal histories and present experiences. Research affords the opportunity to consider those questions in a deep, engaged and (hopefully) systematic way. When heuristic questions arise, heuristic processes of personal and professional inquiry follow (Moustakas, 1990). The challenge is to somehow encapsulate those more personal learning experiences without merely relegating them to schematic or academic conceptualisations. In one sense, as we have seen, learning is evaluated objectively by standing back from it. In another way, deeper, heutagogical (or heuristic) learning (Hase and Kenyon, 2001) is explored through autonomy of thought, action and reflexive experiencing, while recognising (and being able to embrace) the personal and transformational learning that occurs as a result of research engagement. Recently, one research student put it beautifully when she explained that she was '. . . re-entering the snow globe . . .' to walk around in a world that had been shaken up and that she now viewed differently as a result of her personal learning.

Case study 9.2

Tina, another student wrote this personal evaluation at the end of her dissertation:

'My relationship with this research has been symbiotic, a close association of its impact on me and my impact on it. There is no clear divide between these, rather closely interwoven threads connecting one another. This study has been both my enemy and saviour; with passion, joy, despair and frustration being experienced whilst working on it.

In the early stages of the study, it became all consuming, demanding to be fed in terms of time and effort, overtaking my life and leaving me with a sense of loss. I became so focused on producing a dissertation I lost sight of what I really wanted from this research. At the beginning of the study I generally supported the use of therapist self-disclosure, despite being unsure of using this intervention myself; however, as the study progressed, I was aware of a shift in my thoughts as doubts crept in as the shadow side of this intervention began to emerge.

In my personal life, events began to overtake me, causing a reversal in the study taking over my life, to my life overtaking the study. The diagnosis of a serious condition, followed by major surgery for my partner, left me reeling and the research study faltered through worry and sheer exhaustion. Instead of being able to set the study aside, it became my nemesis, invading my thoughts and calling to me back to it even when each day was a battle to get through. An extension was sought to complete this work and engagement in the study was sporadic. I felt alone in my journey as peers surged ahead with their own studies and deadlines.

Gradually, as my partner improved, my thoughts turned back to the research and work began again. The nature of the study changed, providing focus and allowing ongoing worries and concerns to be kept at bay. As I engaged with the

---

research emotions were emerging from an unknown source within me. Unsure of these I spoke about them in supervision, gaining some insight into the unconscious processes driving this research study. During analysis the re-stimulation of a previous traumatic event had led to the re-experiencing of the fear and anxiety attached to it. Connections were made and I am aware this piece work has given me the opportunity to acknowledge my pain, but more importantly allowed the process of self-healing and forgiveness.

As the study concludes its impact is huge, I am aware of mixed emotions, excitement at seeing my research come together and sadness at letting go of what has been such a large part of my life. The completion of this study is significant; it represents an ending, but also a beginning and moving forward from a different personal place than before. Professionally, I feel I have shed some of the naivety I possessed, as well as the rigid thinking regarding therapist self-disclosure, and can make more considered and informed decisions about its use.'

ACTIVITY 9.3

Tina's story is powerful. It reflects her own deep, experiential learning.

- What's your story? What has been your personal learning? What might you need to do with this? You may think about writing a response or capturing your own thoughts and feelings in some other way and sharing these with your peers, tutor, supervisor, personal therapist or those close to you.

Research is a dynamic heutagogic process that is grounded in, and driven by, learner-centred inquiry (Hase and Kenyon, 2001); it does not necessarily finish with the completion of a research product such as a dissertation. It is likely that, in finding answers, you may also have found more questions that have whetted your appetite for further investigation. Questions may have been left partially answered (or not answered at all) and fresh awareness stimulated leading to a quest for further insight. McLeod suggests: *It can be useful to make sense of research as a* **cyclical** *process. Just as with any other form of experiential learning, research moves through stages of planning, action and reflection* (1999, p44; emphasis in original). Here the capacity for reflection to catalyse further and deeper learning (perhaps (although not necessarily) attached to a higher academic award) cannot be overemphasised (see Figure 9.1). The words of the poet TS Eliot (1943) ring true: *We shall not cease from exploration, and the end of all our exploring will be to arrive where we started and know the place for the first time.*

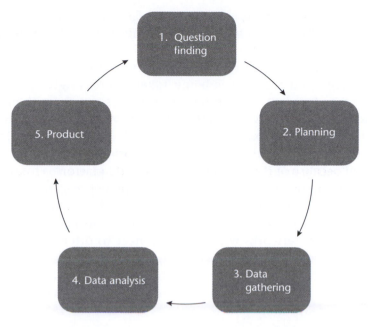

Figure 9.1: Reflection and deeper learning

ACTIVITY 9.4

Sometimes finding, and then refining, an initial research question can be challenging. In reaching the completion of this research cycle, it may be that you have specific and already formulated questions, or a 'hunch' about another research idea that you would like to follow up. Harnessing this momentum is important in recording these ideas, even if you decide not to pursue them immediately. It is also useful to reflect on the 'unanswered' in research work; this adds to the sense of validity and provides a basis for you or others to develop further investigation.

Use the following questions to help.

- What have you learned from the research you are completing?
- What has surprised you?
- What questions are left unanswered?
- What 'hunches' do you have about further research?

For research to be valuable it must have relevance and applicability, and be available in the public domain for others to engage with. Practitioner-based inquiry has the capacity for real depth, passion, wisdom and application because it is in a very real sense grounded in therapeutic realities. Encouragingly, such research is being taken increasingly seriously, and more and more forums where student-researchers can share their findings with others are becoming available. Previously, the danger might have been that research was completed for academic awards that enriched the lives of students, but did little to fulfil its wider social and therapeutic potential because of the paucity of appropriate platforms for dissemination. Counselling research matters. It has the power to generate thinking, learning, debate and change, and there is a range of ways in which student-researchers can share their research findings both formally and informally. Local counselling networks where people meet to offer informal mutual support and learn together are becoming increasingly common. Wenger (2008) describes these learning networks as 'communities of practice'; their potential for mutual learning, which includes the dissemination of research findings, is immeasurable.

Care, however, within this context (as with all contexts) needs to be taken to ensure that research dissemination occurs ethically, and without disclosure of identifiable personal or organisational details. Similarly, it might be appropriate to share research results within organisations, with supervisors, or in group supervision. Different courses in different academic institutions also offer a range of ways in which students can share their work. In some cases, vivas form part of the assessment strategy, while in others students are given the opportunity to lead more informal post-submission seminars in which they discuss their work. Other institutions require students to produce abstracts and presentations on their research, which are then made available in online depositories for wider access and discussion. Higher Education Institutions (HEIs) are increasingly providing excellent conference platforms where students can share their research findings and interact with internationally renowned academic-practitioners. A similar pattern is evident in conferences and symposia organised by professional bodies, which appear increasingly willing to recognise the value of practitioner research. The increase in the range of professional and peer-reviewed journals also affords student-researchers the opportunity to submit, receive feedback on and gain possible publication of their work. Each of these journals has particular criteria for publication that need to be considered. It is often the case that the work produced in dissertations needs to be condensed and a different writing style adopted in order to gain acceptance. Advice on this might be sought from academic tutors and journal editors.

The message however is clear: the research that you have completed is valuable, and should be shared with others in order to stimulate thought, generate debate and inform practice.

ACTIVITY 9.5

Discuss with others ways in which you can disseminate your research findings.

• What advice is given?

Make a plan of action.

• What will you do to share your research results?

ACTIVITY 9.6

As we approach the conclusion of this book, and as you approach the completion of your research journey, reflect on the following questions.

• What has been the impact of the research on your professional learning?
• What are the implications of this learning for wider practice?
• What has been the impact of this research process for you personally?
• What is different now?
• What's next?

CHAPTER SUMMARY

This chapter has outlined the importance of the integrity of research processes and products, and considered ways in which student-researchers might enhance the quality and validity of their work by establishing the transparency of research practices. We have explored ways in which research might demonstrate its credibility and rigour through triangulative methods and challenged readers to evaluate the impact of the research in professional and personal terms. Readers have been asked to consider the unanswered, and new, questions that have arisen, and how these might be processed. Finally, the chapter has examined the importance of research as a vehicle for social and therapeutic good and encouraged student-researchers to commit to the dissemination of their work.

SUGGESTED FURTHER READING

Yardley, L (2009) Demonstrating validity in qualitative psychology, in Smith, J (ed.) *Qualitative Psychology.* London: Sage.

References

Adams, M (2012) Placing ourselves in context: research as a personal narrative, in Bager-Charleson, S (ed.) *Personal Development in Counselling and Psychotherapy*. London: Sage.

Alvesson, M and Sandberg, J (2013) *Constructing Research Questions*. London: Sage.

Atkins, L and Wallace, S (2010) *Qualitative Research in Education*. London: Sage.

Aveline, M (2005) The person of the therapist. *Psychotherapy Research*, 15(3): 155–64.

Aveyard, H (2010) *Doing a Literature Review in Health and Social Care*. Milton Keynes: Open University Press.

Aveyard, H and Sharp, P (2012) *A Beginner's Guide to Evidence Based Practice in Health and Social Care*. Milton Keynes: Open University Press.

Bager-Charleson, S (2010) *Reflective Practice in Counselling and Psychotherapy*. Exeter: Learning Matters.

Bager-Charleson, S (2012) *Personal Development in Counselling and Psychotherapy*. London: Sage.

Banks, JA (2010) The lives and values of researchers: implications for educating citizens in a multicultural society, in Lutterell, W (ed.) *Qualitative Educational Research: Readings in reflexive methodology and transformative practice*. London: Routledge.

Barker, C, Pistrang, N and Elliott, R (2002) *Research Methods in Clinical Psychology*. Chichester: John Wiley and Sons.

Barkham, M, Hardy, GE and Mellor-Clark, J (2010) *Developing and Delivering Practice-Based Evidence: A guide for the psychological therapies*. Chichester: Wiley Blackwell.

Beck, U (1992) *Risk Society: Towards a new modernity*. London: Sage.

Bold, C (2012) *Using Narrative In Research*. London: Sage.

Bolton, G (2010) *Reflective Practice: Writing and professional development*, 3rd edition. London: Sage.

Bond, T (2000) *Standards and Ethics for Counselling in Action*. London: Sage.

Bond, T (2004) *Ethical Guidelines for Researching Counselling and Psychotherapy*. Lutterworth: British Association for Counselling and Psychotherapy. Available at www.bacp.co.uk/research/ethical_guidelines.php

Bond, T (2010) *Standards and Ethics for Counselling in Action*, 3rd edition. London: Sage.

Bond, T and Mitchells, B (2008) *Confidentiality and Record Keeping in Counselling and Psychotherapy*. London: Sage.

Bordin, E (1979) The generalizability of the psychoanalytical concept of the working alliance. *Psychotherapy: Theory Research and Practice*, 16(3): 252–60.

Bower, P (2010) *Evidence Based Practice in Counselling and Psychotherapy*. R2 Information Sheet. Lutterworth: British Association for Counselling and Psychotherapy.

Bowers-Brown, T and Stevens, A (2010) Literature reviews, in Dahlberg, L and McCaig, C (eds) *Practical Research and Evaluation*. London: Sage.

Bowlby, J (1998) *A Secure Base: Clinical applications of attachment theory*. London: Routledge.

Boyatzis, RE (1998) *Transforming Qualitative Information: Thematic analysis and code development*. London: Sage.

Braun, V and Clarke, V (2006) Using thematic analysis in psychology. *Qualitative Research in Psychology*, 3: 77–101.

Bright, G (2011) Does school counselling promote childhood and adolescent resilience? Unpublished MA dissertation. York: York St John University.

British Association for Counselling and Psychotherapy (BACP) (2009) *Accreditation of Training Courses, including the Core Curriculum*, 5th edition. Lutterworth: BACP.

British Association for Counselling and Psychotherapy (BACP) (2010) *Ethical Framework for Good Practice in Counselling & Psychotherapy*. Lutterworth: BACP.

British Association for Counselling and Psychotherapy (BACP) (2012) *Accreditation of Training Courses, including the Core Curriculum, 2009 Scheme, 5th edition – amended 2012*. Lutterworth: BACP. Available at www.bacp.co.uk/admin/structure/files/pdf/11914_atc_scheme_2012.pdf. NB: This document is also known as the 'gold book'.

British Association for Counselling and Psychotherapy (BACP) (2013) *Ethical Framework for Good Practice in Counselling & Psychotherapy*. Rugby: BACP. Available at www.bacp.co.uk/ethical_framework/

Bruner, J (1990) *Acts of Meaning*. Cambridge, MA: Harvard University Press.

Bryman, A (2008) *Social Research Methods*, 3rd edition. Oxford: Oxford University Press.

Carroll, M (2008) *Counselling Supervision*. London: Sage.

Charmaz, K (2006) *Constructing Grounded Theory: A practical guide through qualitative analysis*. London: Sage.

Claringbull, N (2010) *What is Counselling and Psychotherapy?* Exeter: Learning Matters.

Cohen, L, Manion, L and Morrison, K (2007) *Research Methods in Education*, 6th edition. London: Routledge.

Cohen, L, Manion, L and Morrison, K (2011) *Research Methods in Education*, 7th edition. London: Routledge.

Connolly, K and Reid, A (2007) Ethics review for qualitative inquiry: adopting a values-based, facilitative approach. *Qualitative Inquiry*, 13: 1031.

Coolican, H (2013) *Research Methods and Statistics in Psychology*, 5th edition. London: Routledge.

Cooper, M (2008) *Essential Research Findings in Counselling and Psychotherapy*. London: Sage.

Cooper, M (2010) The challenge of counselling and psychotherapy research. *Counselling and Psychotherapy Research*, 10(3): 183–91.

Cooper, M (2011) Meeting the demand for evidence-based practice. *Therapy Today*, 22(4): 10–16.

Cooper, M and McLeod, J (2007) A pluralistic framework for counselling and psychotherapy: Implications for research. *Counselling and Psychotherapy Research*, 7(3): 135–43.

Cooper, M and McLeod, J (2011) *Pluralistic Counselling and Psychotherapy*. London: Sage.

Corrie, S (2010) What is evidence?, in Woolfe, R, Strawbridge, S, Douglas, B and Dryden, W (eds) *Handbook of Counselling Psychology*. London: Sage.

Corsaro, W (2011) *The Sociology of Childhood*. London: Sage.

Cresswell, J (2007) *Qualitative Inquiry and Research Design: Choosing among five approaches*, 2nd edition. London: Sage.

Dallos, R and Vetere, A (2005) *Researching Psychotherapy and Counselling*. Maidenhead: Open University Press.

Davis, N, Clark, CA, O'Brien, M, Plaice, C, Sumpton, K and Waugh, S (2011) *Learning Skills for Nursing Students*. Exeter: Learning Matters.

de Bono, E (1999) *Six Thinking Hats*. London: Penguin.

Denscombe, M (2008) *The Good Research Guide*, 3rd edition. Maidenhead: Open University Press.

Denscombe, M (2010) *Ground Rules for Social Research*, 2nd edition. Maidenhead: Open University Press.

Devereux, G (1967) *From Anxiety to Method in the Behavioral Sciences*. Paris: Mouton.

Drew, P (2009) Conversation analysis, in JA Smith (ed.) *Qualitative Psychology: A practical guide to research methods*. London: Sage.

du Plock, S (2010) The vulnerable researcher, in Bager-Charleson, S (ed.) *Reflective Practice in Counselling and Psychotherapy*. Exeter: Learning Matters.

Eisner, EW (1991) *The Enlightened Eye: Qualitative inquiry and the enhancement of educational practice*. New York: Macmillan.

Eliot, TS (1943) *Four Quartets*. San Diego, CA: Harcourt.

Elliott, A (2008) *Concepts of the Self*. Cambridge: Polity Press.

Elliott, A (2009) *Concepts of the Self*, 2nd edition. Cambridge: Polity Press.

Elliott, R (1993) *Helpful Aspects of Therapy*. Available at http://experiential-researchers.org/index.html

Elliott, R and Freire, E (2010) The effectiveness of person-centred and experiential therapies: a review of the meta-analyses, in Cooper, M,

Watson, JC and Holldampf, D (eds) *Person-centred and Experiential Therapies Work.* Ross-on-Wye: PCCS Books.

Esin, C (2011) Narrative analysis approaches, in Frost, N (ed.) *Qualitative Research Methods in Psychology.* Maidenhead: McGraw-Hill.

Etherington, K (2001) Writing qualitative research: a gathering of selves. *Counselling and Psychotherapy Research*, 1(2): 119–25.

Etherington, K (2004) *Becoming a Reflexive Researcher.* London: Jessica Kingsley.

Etherington, K (2006) Heuristic research as a vehicle for personal and professional development. *Counselling and Psychotherapy Research*, 4(2): 48–63.

Etherington, K (2007) *Trauma, Drug Misuse and Transforming Identities: A life story approach.* London: Jessica Kingsley.

Etherington, K (2009) Life story research: a relevant methodology for counsellors and psychotherapists. *Counselling and Psychotherapy Research*, 9(4): 225–33.

Evaluation Trust (2012) *What is Evaluation?* Retrieved from www.evaluationtrust.org/evaluation/definitions (no longer available).

Evans, C, Connell, J, Barkham, M, Marshall, C and Mellor-Clark, J (2003) Practice-based evidence: benchmarking NHS primary care counselling services at national and local levels. *Clinical Psychology and Psychotherapy*, 10: 374–88.

Farrimond, H (2012) *Doing Ethical Research.* Basingstoke: Palgrave Macmillan.

Finlay, L. (2011) *Phenomenology for Therapists: Researching the lived world.* Chichester: Wiley-Blackwell.

Finlay, L and Evans, K (2009) *Relational-centred Research for Psychotherapists.* Chichester: Wiley-Blackwell.

Finlay, L and Madill, A (2009) Analysis of data, in Finlay, L and Evans, K (eds) *Relational-centred Research for Psychotherapists.* Chichester: Wiley-Blackwell.

Fisher, R (1925) *Statistical Methods for Research Workers.* Edinburgh: Oliver and Boyd.

Flick, U (2010) *An Introduction to Qualitative Research*, 4th edition. London: Sage.

Furlong, A and Cartmel, F (2007) *Young People and Social Change.* Maidenhead: Open University Press.

Gabriel, L (2009) Exploring the researcher–contributor alliance, in Gabriel, L and Casemore, R (eds) *Relational Ethics in Practice: Narratives from counselling and psychotherapy.* London: Routledge.

Green, J (2010) *Creating the Therapeutic Relationship in Counselling and Psychotherapy.* Exeter: Learning Matters.

Guillemin, M and Gillam, L (2004) Ethics, reflexivity and 'ethically important moments' in research. *Qualitative Inquiry*, 10: 261.

Hall, CD (2011) Is how I dress who I am? Unpublished MA dissertation, Leeds.

Hall, C (2012) Developing through the written word, in Rose, C (ed.) *Self Awareness and Personal Development: Resources for psychotherapists and counsellors*. Basingstoke: Palgrave Macmillan.

Halse, C and Honey, A (2007) Rethinking ethics review as institutional discourse. *Qualitative Inquiry*, 13: 336.

Hanley, T, Lennie, C and West, W (2013) *Introducing Counselling and Psychotherapy Research*. London: Sage.

Hase, S and Kenyon, C (2001) *From Andragogy to Heutagogy*. Available at www.psy.gla.ac.uk/~steve/pr/Heutagogy.html

Hawkins, P and Shohet, R (2012) *Supervision in the Helping Professions*, 4th edition. Maidenhead: Open University Press.

Hearn, J (2012) *Theorizing Power*. Basingstoke: Palgrave Macmillan.

Heath, S, Brooks, R, Cleaver, E and Ireland, E (2009) *Researching Young People's Lives*. London: Sage.

Hedges, F (2010) *Reflexivity in Therapeutic Practice*. Basingstoke: Palgrave Macmillan.

Hennink, M, Hutter, I and Bailey, A (2011) *Qualitative Research Methods*. London: Sage.

HM Government (2010) *Indices of Multiple Deprivation*. Available at www.gov.uk/government/uploads/system/uploads/attachment_data/file/6871/1871208.pdf

House, R, Rogers, A and Maidman, J (2011) The bad faith of evidenced-based practice: beyond counsels of despair. *Therapy Today*, 22(6). Available at www.therapytoday.net/article/show/2554/

Howard, A (2000) *Philosophy for Counselling and Psychotherapy*. Basingstoke: Palgrave Macmillan.

Hutchinson, R and Stead, K (1993) *The Rickter Scale*. Available at www.rickterscale.com/

Iphofen, R (2011) Ethical decision making in qualitative research. *Qualitative Research*, 11(4): 443–46.

Jesson, JK, with Matheson, L and Lacey, FM (2012) *Doing Your Literature Review*. London: Sage.

Johns, H (2012) *Personal Development in Counsellor Training*, 2nd edition. London: Sage.

Jones, P and Welch, S (2010) *Rethinking Children's Rights*. London: Continuum.

Kagan, N (1980) Influencing human interaction – eighteen years with IPR, in Hess, AK (ed.) *Psychotherapy Supervision: Theory, research, and practice* (pp262–83). New York: Wiley.

Kellett, M (2010) *Rethinking Children and Research*. London: Continuum.

Kenny, G (2012) An introduction to Moustakas's heuristic method. *Nurse Researcher*, 19(3): 6–11.

Lambert, M (ed.) (2013) *Bergin & Garfield's Handbook of Psychotherapy and Behavior Change*, 6th edition. Hoboken, NJ: Wiley.

Langdridge, D (2007) *Phenomenological Psychology: Theory research and method*. Harlow: Pearson.

Langdridge, D and Hagger-Johnson, G (2009) *Introduction to Research Methods and Data Analysis in Psychology*. Harlow: Pearson Prentice Hall.

Lapworth, P and Sills, C (2011) *Integration in Counselling and Psychotherapy*, 2nd edition. London: Sage.

Larkin, M, Watts, S and Clifton, E (2006) Giving voice and making sense in Interpretative Phenomenological Analysis. *Qualitative Research in Psychology*, 3: 102–20.

Layder, D (2013) *Doing Excellent Small-Scale Research*. London: Sage.

Lincoln, YS and Guba, EG (1985) *Naturalistic Inquiry*. Beverly Hills, CA: Sage.

Lincoln, YS and Tierney, WG (2004) Qualitative research and institutional review boards. *Qualitative Inquiry*, 10: 219.

Luca, M (2009) A therapist's portrait of a clinical encounter with a somatizer, in Finlay, L and Evans, K (eds) *Relational-centred Research for Psychotherapists*. Chichester: Wiley-Blackwell.

Macfarlane, B (2010) Values and virtues in qualitative research, in Savin-Baden, M and Major, CH (eds) *New Approaches to Qualitative Research*. London: Routledge.

Mair, M (1989) *Between Psychology and Psychotherapy: A poetics of experience*. London: Routledge.

May, T and Perry, B (2011) *Social Research and Reflexivity*. London: Sage.

McArthur, K (2011) RCTs: a personal experience. *Therapy Today*, 22(7): 24–5.

McDonnell, L, Stratton, P, Butler, S and Cape, N (2012) Developing research informed practitioners – an organisational perspective. *Counselling and Psychotherapy Research*, 12(3): 167–77.

McLeod, J (1999) *Practitioner Research in Counselling*. London: Sage.

McLeod, J (2007a) *Doing Counselling Research*, 2nd edition. London: Sage.

McLeod, J (2007b) *Qualitative Research in Counselling and Psychotherapy*. London: Sage.

McLeod, J (2010) *Case Study Research in Counselling and Psychotherapy*. London: Sage.

McLeod, J (2011a) We need more good quality non-RCT evidence. *Therapy Today*, 22(7): 36–7.

McLeod, J (2011b) *Qualitative Research in Counselling and Psychotherapy*, 2nd edition. London: Sage.

McLeod, J (2013a) Research on person-centred counselling, in Mearns, D, and Thorne, B with McLeod, J, *Person-centred Counselling in Action*, 4th edition. London: Sage.

McLeod, J (2013b) *Introduction to Research in Counselling and Psychotherapy*. London: Sage.

McLeod, J, Elliott, R and Wheeler, S (2010) *Training Counsellors and Psychotherapists in Research Skills: A manual of resources*. Lutterworth: British Association for Counselling and Psychotherapy.

McNiff, J (2013) *Action Research: Principles and practice*, 3rd edition. London: Routledge.

Mearns, D and Cooper, M (2005) *Working at Relational Depth in Counselling and Psychotherapy*. London: Sage.

Mearns, D and Thorne, B (2000) *Person-centred Therapy Today*. London: Sage.

Mearns, D and Thorne, B (2007) *Person-centred Counselling in Action*, 3rd edition. London: Sage.

Mellor-Clark, J and Barkham, M (2012) Using the CORE system to support service quality development, in Feltham, C and Horton, I (eds) *The Sage Handbook of Counselling and Psychotherapy*. London: Sage.

Merry, T (1999) *Learning and Being in Person-centred Counselling*. Ross-on-Wye: PCCS Books.

Miles, J and Banyard, P (2007) *Understanding and Using Statistics in Psychology: A practical introduction*. London: Sage.

Mills, CW (2010) On intellectual craftsmanship, in Luttrell, W (ed.) *Qualitative Educational Research*. London: Routledge.

Mitchells, B and Bond, T (2010) *Essential Law for Counsellors and Psychotherapists*. London: Sage.

Moran, P (2011) Bridging the gap between research and practice in counselling and psychotherapy training: learning from trainees. *Counselling and Psychotherapy Research*, 11(3): 171–8.

Morrall, P (2008) *The Trouble With Therapy: Sociology and psychotherapy*. Maidenhead: Open University Press.

Moss, B (2007) *Values*. Lyme Regis: Russell House.

Moustakas, C (1990) *Heuristic Research: Design, methodology and applications*. Thousand Oaks, CA: Sage.

Muncey, T (2011) *Creating Autoethnographies*. London: Sage.

Muran, J, Castonguay, L and Strauss, B (2010) A brief introduction to psychotherapy research, in Castonguay, L, Muran, J, Angus, L, Hayes, J, Ladany, N and Anderson, T (eds) *Bringing Psychotherapy Research to Life*. Washington, DC: American Psychological Association.

Murray, M (2009) Narrative psychology, in Smith, JA (ed.) *Qualitative Psychology: A practical guide to research methods*. London: Sage.

National Institute for Health and Care Excellence (NICE) (2013a) *NICE Journals and Databases*. Available at www.evidence.nhs.uk/nhs-evidence-content/journals-and-databases (accessed 9 July 2013).

National Institute for Health and Care Excellence (NICE) (2013b) *Depression in Adults* (Update) (CG90). Available at www.nice.org.uk/CG90 (accessed 14 August 2013).

National Society for the Prevention of Cruelty to Children (NSPCC) (2012) *Gillick Competency and Fraser Guidelines*, NSPCC factsheet. Available at www.nspcc.org.uk/inform/research/questions/gillick_wda61289.html

O'Donnell, M and Vallance, K (2012) Supervisors self-awareness. *Therapy Today*, 23(5): 35–7.

Oliver, P (2012) *Succeeding With Your Literature Review: A handbook for students*. Milton Keynes: Open University Press.

Owens, P, Springwood, B and Wilson, M (2012) *Creative Ethical Practice in Counselling and Psychotherapy*. London: Sage.

Palmer, S, Dainow, S and Milner, P (1996) *Counselling: The BAC counselling reader*. London: Sage.

Parker, I (2005) *Qualitative Psychology: Introducing radical research.* Maidenhead: Open University Press.

Pashler, H and Wagenmakers, E (2012) Editors' introduction to the special section on replicability in psychological science. *Perspectives on Psychological Science*, 7(6): 528–30.

Pezalla, AE, Pettigrew, J and Miller-Day, M (2012) Researching the researcher-as-instrument: an exercise in interviewer self-reflexivity. *Qualitative Research*, 12: 165–85.

Popper, K (1972) *Objective Knowledge.* Oxford: Oxford University Press.

Proctor, G (2006) Therapy: opium of the masses, or help for those who least need it, in Proctor, G, Cooper, M, Sanders, P and Malcolm, B (eds) *Politicising the Person-centred Approach: An agenda for social change.* Ross-on-Wye: PCCS Books.

Proctor, G and Keys, S (2013) Ethics in practice in person-centred therapy, in Cooper, M, O'Hara, M, Schmid, P and Wyatt, G (eds) *The Handbook of Person-centred Psychotherapy and Counselling*, 2nd edition. Basingstoke: Palgrave Macmillan.

Ransome, P (2013) *Ethics and Values in Social Research.* Basingstoke: Palgrave Macmillan.

Rawls, J (1971) *A Theory of Justice.* London: Harvard University Press.

Reason, P and Heron, J (2003) Co-operative inquiry, in Smith, J, Harre, R and Van Langenhove, L (eds) *Rethinking Methods in Psychology.* London: Sage.

Reason, P and Riley, S (2009) Co-operative inquiry: an action research practice, in Smith, JA (ed.) *Qualitative Psychology: A practical guide to research methods.* London: Sage.

Reeves, A (2013) *An Introduction to Counselling and Psychotherapy.* London: Sage.

Reid, K, Flowers, P and Larkin, M (2005) Exploring the lived experience: an introduction to Interpretative Phenomenological Analysis. *The Psychologist*, 18: 20–3.

Ridley, D (2012) *The Literature Review*, 2nd edition. London: Sage.

Riessman, CK (2008) *Narrative Methods for the Human Sciences.* Thousand Oaks, CA: Sage.

Ritchie, J and Lewis, J (2003) *Qualitative Research Practice: A guide for social science students and researchers.* London: Sage.

Roberts, J (2009) *Youth Work Ethics.* Exeter: Learning Matters.

Roddam, H and Skeat, J (2010) What does EBP mean to speech and language therapists?, in Roddam, HSJ (ed.) *Embedding Evidence Based Practice in Speech and Language Therapy: International examples.* London: Wiley. Available at http://onlinelibrary.wiley.com/book/10.1002/978047068 6584

Rogers, CR (1951) *Client-centred Therapy.* Boston, MA: Houghton Mifflin.

Rogers, CR (1967) *On Becoming a Person: A therapist's view of psychotherapy.* London: Constable.

Ropers-Huilman, R and Winters, KY (2010) Imagining intersectionality and the spaces in between: theories and processes of socially transformative knowing, in Savin-Baden, M and Major, CH (eds) *New Approaches to Qualitative Research: Wisdom and uncertainty.* London: Routledge.

Rose, C and Worsley, R (2012) Thinking about the self, in Rose, C (ed.) *Self Awareness and Personal Development: Resources for psychotherapists and counsellors.* Basingstoke: Palgrave Macmillan.

Rowan, J and Jacobs, M (2011) *The Therapist's Use of Self.* Maidenhead: Open University Press.

Ryan, GW and Bernard, HR (2000) Data management and analysis methods, in Denzin, NK and Lincoln, YS (eds) *Handbook of Qualitative Research,* 2nd edition. London: Sage.

Sackett, DL, Rosenberg, WMC, Muir, JA, Hayes, RB and Richardson, WS (1996) Evidence based medicine: what it is and what it is not. *British Medical Journal,* 312(7023): 71–2.

Sanders, P and Wilkins, P (2010*) First Steps in Practitioner Research: A guide to understanding and doing research in counselling and health and social care.* Ross-on-Wye: PCCS Books.

Savin-Baden, M and Major, CH (2013) *Qualitative Research: The essential guide to theory and practice.* London: Routledge.

Schirato, T, Danaher, G and Webb, J (2012) *Understanding Foucault: A critical introduction,* 2nd edition. London: Sage.

Schön, DA (1983) *The Reflective Practitioner.* New York: Basic Books.

Scruton, R (1995) *Short History of Modern Philosophy,* 2nd edition. London: Routledge.

Shinebourne, P (2011) Interpretative Phenomenological Analysis, in Frost, N (ed.) *Qualitative Research Methods in Psychology.* Maidenhead: McGraw-Hill.

Silverman, D (2009) *Interpreting Qualitative Data,* 3rd edition. London: Sage.

Smith, JA and Osborn, M (2009) Interpretative Phenomenological Analysis, in Smith, JA (ed.) *Qualitative Psychology: A practical guide to research methods.* London: Sage.

Smith, JA, Flowers, P and Larkin, M (2009) *Interpretative Phenomenological Analysis.* London: Sage.

Smith, M (2010) Ethics and research governance, in Dahlberg, L and McCaig, C (eds) *Practical Research and Evaluation.* London: Sage.

Spinelli, E (2010) *The Interpreted World: An introduction to phenomenological psychology,* 2nd edition. London: Sage.

Spradley, JP (1980) *Participant Observation.* New York: Rinehart and Winston.

Stewart, W (2005) *The A–Z of Counselling Theory and Practice.* Cheltenham: Nelson Thornes.

Timulak, L (2008) *Research in Psychotherapy and Counselling.* London: Sage.

Timulak, L and Creaner, M (2010) Qualitative meta-analysis of outcomes of person-centred and experiential psychotherapies, in Cooper, M, Watson, JC and Holldampf, D (eds) *Person-centred and Experiential Therapies Work.* Ross-on-Wye: PCCS Books.

van Rijn, B (2010) Evaluating our practice, in Bager-Charleson, S (ed.) *Reflective Practice in Counselling and Psychotherapy.* Exeter: Learning Matters.

Wenger, E (2008) *Communities of Practice.* Cambridge: Cambridge University Press.

Westergaard, J (2013) Supervising the supervisor: transforming counselling practice, in Reid, H and Westergaard, J, *Effective Supervision for Counsellors.* London: Learning Matters.

Wheeler, S and Elliott, R (2008) What do counsellors and psychotherapists need to know about research? *Counselling and Psychotherapy Research*, 8(2): 133–5.

Wheeler, S and Hicks, C (2000) The role of research in the professional development of counselling, in Palmer, S, Dainow, S and Milner, P (eds) *The BAC Counselling Reader.* London: Sage.

White, P (2009) *Developing Research Questions: A guide for social scientists.* Basingstoke: Palgrave Macmillan.

Widdowson, M (2012) Perceptions of psychotherapy trainees of psychotherapy research. *Counselling and Psychotherapy Research*, 12(3): 178–86.

Wilkins, P (2010) Researching in a person-centred way, in Cooper, M, Watson, JC and Holldampf, D (eds) *Person-centred and Experiential Therapies Work.* Ross-on-Wye: PCCS Books.

Willig, C (2009) Conversation analysis, in Smith, JA (ed.) *Qualitative Psychology: A practical guide to research methods.* London: Sage.

Wosket, V (2011) *The Therapeutic Use of Self.* London: Routledge.

Wright, J and Bolton, G (2012) *Reflective Writing in Counselling and Psychotherapy.* London: Sage.

Yardley, L (2009) Demonstrating validity in qualitative psychology, in Smith, J (ed.) *Qualitative Psychology.* London: Sage.

Yates, S (2004) *Doing Social Science Research.* London: Sage.

Zahavi, D (2008) *Subjectivity and Selfhood: Investigating the first-person perspective.* London: MIT Press.

Index